Homile
Persuasive

Dr. Stan DeKoven   Ernest Weaver

VISION PUBLISHING
1520 Main Street, Suite C, Ramona, CA 92065
(760) 789-4700   Fax: (760) 789-3023

Acknowledgment

We humbly acknowledge Dr. Ken Chant, a prince of preachers for his input and example, along with my Pastor, Dr. Joseph Bohac, for being a most inspirational preacher of God's Word.

Artwork by Ernest Weaver © 1999

Cartoons on pages 37, 45, 48, 58, 96, 106, 159, 174, 195, 210, 219, and 229
are from the book
Church People, Funny Side Up
by Ernest Weaver
© 1991 Weaver Publishing

Used by permission.

Other cartoons were created for this textbook.
and are dedicated to the premise that some
preachers take themselves much too seriously.
Cartoons © 1999 Ernest Weaver

ISBN # 1-931178-77-1

© 1994 Vision Publishing
No reproduction without permission from the publisher.
International rights reserved.

Second Edition 2004

Preaching: Art or Science?

What makes for good preaching? Many different opinions could be advanced, depending on the perception and frame of reference of the hearer. Some would say that preaching should be standardized, such as a three point sermon format. Others would say that good preaching must stimulate the intellect; others prefer a focus on the emotions. Actually, an effective preacher will do both. But anointed preaching will always touch the spirit of the hearer, will motivate people to become conformed to the image of Christ.

Funk and Wagnall's Standard Encyclopedia Dictionary (1972) defines preaching as "To advocate or recommend urgently; to proclaim or expound upon; to preach the gospel. To deliver, to give advice, especially in an officious manner."

From this definition we can infer that preaching should advocate or recommend urgently and expound upon the Gospel of Jesus Christ. True preachers advise men and women of their moral obligations before God. Good preaching would thus be any proclamation of the Good News that will stir people with the truth of the claims of Jesus Christ. In this sense, form follows function. That is, the methodology applied should be based upon the purpose of the preaching.

As pastors, teachers, evangelists, or men and women in training for the same, the proclamation of the Word of God is an essential part of our overall ministry. So important is the ministry of the Word that even the needs of the poor widows were considered secondary to it (and to prayer). [Acts 6:3-4] Thus, it must be a primary focus of our calling as men and women of God.

In this book you will learn some of the most important aspects of effective and persuasive preaching, provided to you with keen insight by some master preachers. Each contributor has many years of outstanding preaching and teaching experience, in a variety of fields and settings. Much can be learned from these pages which, when judiciously applied, will enhance the student's ability to communicate the dynamic truth of the glorious Gospel of Christ. As with anything, without practical application the learning process would be incomplete. Our prayer is that application will be made to the "whosoever will" in the highways and hedges of the world.

Homiletics
Persuasive and Effective Preaching

Table of Contents

Preaching: Art or Science?... 5
Introduction to Part One 11

Part 1 Speaking in Public 13

Chapter One Physical Elements of Speech 15
   Body Language 17
      Gesturing 17
      The Voice 22
      Speaking with Grace 28
   Use the Voice Effectively 32
      Some ways to Emphasize a Point 34

Chapter 2 The Formal Platform Speech 37
   Speech Substance 41
   Informal Conference Room Speech 45
   The Speech of Introduction 46
   The After-Dinner Speech 47
   Listener's Laws for Speech Phraseology 49
   Listener's Laws for Speech Delivery 51
   Suggested Projects 53
   Developing Courage and Confidence 55
      Self-Confidence through Preparation 57
      How Famous Speakers Prepared their Addresses 59
   Some ways of planning a speech 59
   The Improvement of Memory 60
   Keeping the Audience Awake 61
   The Secret of Good Delivery 62
      Platform Presence 62
      How to Open a Talk 64
      How to Close a Talk 65
      Make Your Meaning Clear 66
      How to be Impressive and Convincing 66

Part II Homiletics - The Art of Preaching 69

Chapter 3 The Preacher 71
- The Personal Qualities of a Good Preacher 73
- Some basic Keys to Good Health 77
- Basic Requirements for Christian Ministry 77
  - Personal Qualities 79
  - Personal problems 92
  - Voice interlude 97
  - *Some appropriate quotations:* 98
    - On Long Sermons 99
    - On Rambling Sermons 100

Chapter 4 The Direction for a Sermon 103
- Five parts to good communication 103
- The Whole Counsel of God 106
- The "Hobby Horse" Syndrome 107
- The "Final Answer" Syndrome 108
- Give the Lord your Best 108

Chapter 5 Preparing a Message 111
- Step One: Think and Pray about the Theme 111
- Step Two: Develop that Theme 111
- Make an Outline 112
- Stories: Meat on the Skeleton 114
- Choosing a Scripture Text 115
- Advantages of Finding the Right Text for the Message 116
- General Principles about Preaching 117
  - What should I preach about? 117
  - Topics that should get attention 118
- Particular Principles 118
- Precautions in the Choice of Texts 120
- Interpretation of the Text 122

Chapter 6 The Theme 127
- Gathering Sermon Material 130
- Arranging Sermon Material 132
- Characteristics of a Good Arrangement 132
- Assembling the Sermon 133
- The Body of the Message 133
- The Divisions 134

Chapter 7 Types of Sermons 139
   1. Running Commentary 139
   2. Structured Exposition 140
   3. Topical 142
   Life Situations.. 142
   Biographical 143
   Bible Reading 144
   Textual 145
   Question and Answer 145
   The Expository Sermon.. 145

Chapter 8 How to Prepare an Expository Sermon 151
   The Purpose of Expository Preaching 153
   The Value of Expository Preaching...................................... 153
      What Should a Preacher Know? 154
      The Danger of "Harping on the Same String"................... 155
      The Benefits of Expository Preaching for the Preacher 156
      The Benefits of Expository Preaching for the
      Congregation.. 155
      Reasons for Scarcity 156
      Speaking as an Oracle of God 160
      Sample of an Expository Outline 164
      Distinctions in the Expository Form 166
      Whole Book 167
      Short Book Exposition 167
      Long Book Exposition.. 168
      Chapter Exposition 169
      Short Passage Exposition 169
   Qualities Requisite for Success as an Expositor.................. 171
   Vocal Expression and the Expository Method...................... 175

Chapter 9 Sermon Divisions 178
   The Theme 178
   The Introduction.. 181
   Steps in the Main Division of a Sermon............................... 184
      When to Make your Divisions 188
      Three Basic Methods of Making Sermon Divisions:......... 188
   Basic Guidelines for Sermon Structure................................. 189
   Making a Sermon Interesting.. 190
   Sermon Conclusions 196

Chapter 10 Bible Study Methods 201
   The Deductive Approach. 201
   The Inductive Approach 202
      Characteristics of the Inductive Method. 202
      Procedure for Inductive Study 203
      The Value of an Inductive Chart 207
      Tools Necessary for Inductive Study 208
      Relation to Expository Preaching 209
   Tools for Bible Research 216
      Keeping a Homiletics File 218

Chapter 11 Sermon Outline Methods 221
   Dynamics of Good Outlining 223
   Types of Sermon Outlines 225
      The Character Outline Method 225
      The Key-Word Method 226
      The Pictorial Outline Method 227
      The Narrative Outline Method 229
      The Synthetic Outline Method 233
      The Contrast Outline Method 234
      The Chapter Outline Method 235
      The Verse Outline Method 237
      The Phrase Outline Method 239

Chapter 12 The Apostle Paul 241
   Exhortations from Paul to Timothy 241
   Exhortations from Other Letters by Paul 244

Annotated Bibliography 249

Bibliography 257

Introduction to part one: "Public Speaking"

Our first section is a study on the practical mechanics of public speaking. While it may be argued that the most important aspect of preaching is the ability to hear from God and have a clear and true message, it is also vital to learn to speak with skill and poise. The message is more important than the medium, but the message must have a means of delivery. God can communicate to people through angels, through the Bible, through circumstances, miracles, and even by direct revelation. But *"God chose the foolishness of preaching to save them that believe."* [1] That is, God in His wisdom chose to use imperfect people to communicate truth to imperfect people; not exclusively, but predominantly.

We have a glorious message about the perfect plan of our infinitely awesome Father. We are told to declare the truth and reflect the spirit of Jesus, the perfect man and Son of God. Yet we do so as fallible humans.

Our objective is never to seek to make the message seem greater than it is, for that is impossible. God is perfect. Heaven could not be better, and hell could not be more horrible. We cannot make eternity longer or infinity greater. All we can do is diminish the message through carnal living, or through poor communication.

In preaching, we communicate through words, verbal expressions, body language, appearance, and attitude. When we use accurate words (which effectively express logical and biblical ideas), we are reflecting the spirit of the Gospel. The Bible was not birthed in human logic, but it is logical. Wisdom is intellect in proper subjection to the Spirit. Obviously, if we use poor grammar, sloppy enunciation, and meaningless gestures, we can only diminish the communication.

Have you ever heard a music group with drums and music so loud that the words were indistinguishable? They may communicate a feeling, but the message is lost. So it is with preachers who do not speak well. Poor grammar is distracting, as well as unclear. Mispronounced words, misused words, aimless gestures, poor posture, vocal monotone, and weak enunciation all

---
[1] I Corinthians 1:21

diminish the effectiveness of the message. It is not "carnal" to focus on the practical skills of delivery, because only excellence can accurately convey the full impact of the Word of God. *"We have this treasure* (the message and Spirit of Jesus Christ) *in earthen vessels* (physical presentation)..*that the excellency of the power may be of God, and not of us."* [2]

Ernest E. Weaver

---

[2] II Corinthians 4:7

Part One

Speaking in Public

by Lola L. Mitchell
with Ernest Weaver

Chapter One

Physical Elements of Speech

Body Language for Public Speakers

Assume the Position for Effective Speaking.

Many of the people in the audience had read books by the noted author, and were eagerly anticipating his first appearance in their city. They applauded enthusiastically when he was introduced. But he was not far into his prepared sermon when he realized that he was not connecting with the listeners. He was well prepared. He knew his subject, but the monotonous tone of his voice and the sight of his stooped shoulders were so distracting that soon most of the people were staring at the ceiling and letting their minds wander to a multitude of imaginary destinations. His only gesture was an occasional flip of the left hand, which seemed to suggest that it had a mind of its own, and it had no idea what was going on in the message either. When he perceived the increasing lack of response, his countenance fell further, and he projected even more uneasiness. "Maybe I should have stayed in the pizza business..." he muttered to himself as he mercifully finished his discourse.

[handwritten: Some people use the pulpit to be noticed. Confidence to be yourself.]

Body Language

Stand and walk with the bearing of a leader. To help yourself, try to picture in your mind a noble Indian chief coming to deliver a message of defiance. See him standing erect and tall. His shoulders are thrown back, and his head is held high. His chest is expanded, and his body is ready to act. He has the dignity and poise of a leader. He is the picture of assured confidence. Remember that your body language is your first point on communication with your audience. People will be less likely to have confidence in your message if they pick up on negative non-verbal signals from the speaker.

Keep in mind that you may speak and act like a leader or like a slave. If you form the habit of speaking with a sagged body and deflated chest, that position will diminish the effectiveness of your presentation. Your posture and demeanor also affects your mental attitude. If you speak weakly, your thoughts will seem to lack clarity.

From the letters of the Apostle Paul, we notice that he was a much stronger writer than a public speaker. His critics claimed that *"his letters... are weighty and powerful, but his bodily presence is weak, and his speech contemptible."* (II Corinthians 10:10) History records that Paul was apparently a frail man with a hunched back. He was not physically able to stand erect and tall, although his message was powerful. Peter and Apollos were more effective public speakers, even though Paul was far more intellectual and spiritually mature.

The general purpose of public speaking is to influence people with your ideas and information. This is especially true of preaching. Your goal should be to lead people toward a close walk with the Lord by communicating Biblical truth. If you are going to influence people, you must first win them to yourself. You need to appear confident, but not pretentious. You need to be yourself, but also be dignified. You need to be personable and natural without being silly.

Communicate a positive attitude. Stand erect resting your weight almost equally on both feet, but with one foot slightly advanced, the arms held loosely, the shoulders thrown back. Keep your head straight, and hold your stomach in, especially if there is too much of it. Let the position be easy and in no sense stiff. You are now in the best position for speaking to an audience.

Gesturing Body langge is important

Gesturing is the movement of hands and arms to express meaning. It is an important means of strengthening communication if it is done well. A gesture used at the right moment is a great visual aid. It often can give just the right touch to convey a particular shade of meaning. For example, an extended arm and pointing finger can draw attention to the future, or to a specific point. Throwing up your hands as a gesture usually expresses helplessness and despair. There is no end to the list of gestures and their meaning. You probably use most of them in normal speaking.

Using your hands and arms

- ☐ Do not be stiff, but be careful not to overdo gesturing. Remember that when you over-use gestures, you detract from their power to emphasize.

- ☐ Do not make awkward gestures. There are plenty of natural and common gestures, so do not invent new ones so that you look silly.

- ☐ When you gesture, be sure that your hands and arms can be seen. For instance, do not keep your hands down almost to your knees.

- ☐ Bring your arm up so that everyone can see it. Otherwise people will think your upper arm and shoulders are jerking.

- ☐ Avoid being overly dramatic.

What to do with your hands when they are not in use.

- ☐ Do not keep them perpetually hanging by your side.
- ☐ You can let one arm hang at your side and hold the other in front of you, waist high.
- ☐ Do not continuously move your hands from one position to another. Keep them in one place for sometime.

Facial Expressions

- ☐ Never frown. It is easy to unconsciously slip into a frown when you are nervous or intensely in earnest about what you are saying.
- ☐ Do not let your face be rigid. Relax.
- ☐ Use your face to express natural expressions.

- On the other hand, neither should you grin continuously. That is a sign of nervousness. Smile pleasantly when it is appropriate. Your face can be your most effective and expressive tools in body language. Warm and natural smiles are also quite contagious.

Some Rules for Bodily Movement :

Never do anything that looks unnatural before an audience. It may attract the wrong kind of attention, or detract from your message. A gesture which seems unnatural makes the audience uncomfortable. Poor gestures or body movements will detract from what you are saying.

Today, in this era of cordless microphones and better technology, it is possible to move around the platform, or even into the audience. This can be effective, if it is done rarely, and correctly. Never move to an individual if it would be negative or embarrassing. A positive movement, such as taking a hand to show compassion, can punctuate the thought better than a word picture.

Walking around excessively makes you look nervous or confused, and it will communicate the same to the people. On the other hand, if you stand squarely behind the pulpit all the time, you will look as if you are bound to a set of notes. Standing to one side or the other removes a visual barrier between you and the people, and can make them feel more at ease.

Billy Sunday was a baseball player in the days before prohibition. He became a zealous preacher, and was famous for his athletic and energetic preaching style. He would even jump over the pulpit to emphasize a point. Many people came just out of curiosity, but they often got the message in the process.

Some movements to avoid

☐ **Leaning**
If you lean too much to one side, people will feel uncomfortable.

☐ **Swaying**
Never sway from side to side or teeter back and forth.

☐ **Shifting weight**
Some people stand on one foot, then the other. This makes an audience nervous.

☐ **Scraping feet on the floor**
It is irritating to see a speaker dragging and scraping his feet along the floor. In some settings, it can even make distracting noise.

☐ **Sagging hip**
Do not stand as if you had one hip out of joint.

☐ **Stooped shoulders**
Do not act as if you were lazy or all tired out with your shoulders slouched.

☐ **Standing with feet too close together or too far apart**
When you stand with feet far apart you look clumsy, awkward, and ungainly. If you stand with them too close together, you will look like a soldier at attention.

☐ **Pacing back and forth**
You may walk about but be sure and stand in one spot for awhile so you will not give the impression that you are in a fenced enclosure trying to get out.

☐ **Sitting on a desk or leaning on the pulpit**
If you are nervous, you'll be tempted to lean on or cling to the pulpit or desk until it will appear as if you have no physical strength.

Always try to be at ease and have self-confidence. Then you can control yourself and your audience. Good body language is essential to positive communication. Remember, we have the most wonderful and important message. In the world to share.

Exercises to be used in class or personal practice:

(Clench right fist, bring it down sharply and say the following:) "I defy any man to find one touch of dishonesty in my record!"
(Extend both arms to half-lowered position, open hands loosely, hold palms upward and toward hearers and say:) "That is the whole story. There is no more."
(Extend the right arm somewhat to the right and point with the index finger and say:) "Someday, Jesus will return, and every eye shall see Him!"
(Aim your right index finger to the sky, then bring it down to point to the audience) "Where will **you** spend eternity?"

Voice

Develop a Pleasing, Impressing Voice.

Many doors are closed to the twanger, squeaker, boomer, grinder, whisperer, shrieker, and whiner.

Relax!

Let go o o o o o o o o o. Relaxation fosters a calmer spirit, improved poise and better thinking. Hence you gain many things besides a better voice. Anyone who forces his voice by speaking too loudly pays a heavy price for it. Sometimes when the voice is coerced too far it becomes permanently damaged. Relaxing the heavy throat muscles (those principally used in chewing and swallowing) help to make the tone passage free and unrestricted.

Exercise:
- Tighten your jaw and throat and say, "get out of here," then relax your throat and say the same thing. You should be able to easily discern the difference.
- Clench your teeth, and say, "I love everybody I know." Notice that it sounds disingenuous.
- Relax your whole body, drop your jaw loosely and say "wah, wah, wah", for a few

minutes and see how you are relaxed from tenseness.
- ☐ Yawn.

Learn to breathe properly

Breathe from the diaphragm, not with the chest heaving. Defective breathing affects the voice unfavorably. Too much effort from the throat gives a labored, strained effect. It restricts the voice, and constricts the nasal passages which are necessary for resonating tone. You must breathe deeply to support the tone well. Make breathing deep by the use of the diaphragm (the muscle under the lungs).

Learn to use the diaphragm.

Watch yourself in a large mirror carefully and try to breathe with your diaphragm when standing erect. Your shoulders should not rise at all. Put your hands over your stomach and pant vigorously through your mouth while saying "yuh, yuh". You will feel your stomach pushing in as you make the sound.

Train your ear.

You need to have a clear mental picture of the quality of voice you wish to develop. Listen to other people when they are speaking. Notice that the most pleasing and appealing voices are generally low in pitch. Note that we always tend to judge people, not only by the words they use, but also by the way in which they speak. Now listen to yourself, and make an evaluation. Does your tone of voice communicate the joy of the Lord, or empathy? Do you sound nervous, harsh, or lazy?

Speak with the appropriate volume.

One of the most disagreeable things in the world is to have to try to hear a person who habitually speaks too softly, or fails to enunciate clearly. The correct volume depends upon the place of meeting, and the equipment used. If a speaker has a good public address system and still shouts, he will not be effective. He will come across as either harsh or nervous. A good sound system will make the speaker sound natural, as if he were speaking to you personally and directly. It is not meant to blast the listener with overpowering sound to manipulate emotions. That is basically what rock music does. Good music and good speaking have a much more subtle influence.

There are many older preachers around today who have destroyed their voice with years of loud preaching. In their latter years, they struggle to speak, or they have a hoarse, raspy voice. It's not because they were loud, but because they spoke with poor breath support, and wrong technique.

One of the great preachers of history was George Whitefield, an 18th century English evangelist who did much of his preaching in America. He not only had a good mind and a clear Biblical message: He was also a strong speaker with a well-trained voice. Whitefield would often preach three times a day, and his sermons would average two hours in length. He usually spoke outdoors to crowds of up to thirty thousand people at a time. It is said that he could be clearly understood nearly a mile away. Benjamin Franklin was his friend and admirer, although he never became a Christian. Whitefield was called "the silver-tongued orator."

When you speak outside, there are no walls to reflect the sound. The sound waves keep going into the atmosphere. Apparently, Jesus Christ had a strong speaking voice, because He also spoke to large outdoor crowds without a sound system. There are people today who are rich and famous singers who might have trouble filling a one-seater outhouse with sound without their megawatt amplifiers and sophisticated studio microphones.

Develop resonance in your voice.

A straight tone is weak, colorless and unpleasant. The effect of a flat (non-resonating) vocal tone is similar to the effect of reverberation in a room. To hear the difference, sing outside in a open field, and then sing in the shower. Notice that you sound so much better in the shower. The reason is simple acoustics. The sound of your voice in the shower is bouncing around in a confined space, and it sounds more full and rich. Do not rush out to find a recording contract to sign. Most of us sound pretty good in the shower.

Try humming until you feel the vibrating response in your lips, nose, and chest. Do it often. When you say "mmmmm," the tone you are generating will hit your closed lips, but will come out through your nose. If your vocal chords and nasal passages are resonating (vibrating), your lips will tickle. When they tickle, open your mouth with an "ahhhh", maintaining the vibrations. Hum up and down a musical scale and direct your tones forward in your mouth. Tones that are too restricted (from the throat) are called "guttural". Work for a pleasant quality.

The quality of your voice reflects your personality and emotional state. Cultivate a voice which conveys a sense of warmth and friendliness. Make your voice match your age. A mature person should never speak in a childish treble. Conversely, a young person seems incongruous if he sounds like a sports announcer.

Bad Voice Techniques:

Breathiness:	Caused by failure to bring vocal chords closely enough together.
Metallic:	Too much energy in making tone and tight throat muscles.
Thinness:	Cause by lack of resonance.
Hoarseness:	Caused by a virus, bacteria infection, or by straining the voice.

Falsetto: Caused by getting resonance from the back part of the hard palate.
Weakness: Caused by too little breath and vigor.
Nasality: Caused by restricting the nasal passages where much of the natural resonance of the voice takes place.
Talking "through the nose":
Actually, some of the sound of a good voice comes through the nose. If you doubt that, talk or sing while blocking your nose with your fingers. You are not really talking "through your nose." Actually, you are doing the opposite. The tone is so flat because the nasal passages resonate the tone, and are necessary for a good quality vocal sound.

Vocal Pitch

Keep your voice pleasantly low. You should have a voice range of about two octaves. If your voice is too high or too low, you are under physical strain and you are handicapping yourself.

Good speakers and actors have low-pitched, resonant voices because their voices carry better and are kind to ears of listeners. Since the pitch (frequency of vibration) is determined by the length of the vocal cords, taller people have a natural advantage. Their necks are longer. We raise or lower the pitch of our voices by adjusting the length of the vocal cords with our neck muscles. We can train ourselves to stretch them more as we speak or sing.

High-pitched voices are more likely to irritate the listener, especially if they are shrill or forced. That's why a person who is suddenly terrified will emit a very high, shrill sound called a "scream." Fear causes the muscles to constrict, including the neck muscles. Stage fright will do the same thing, so you cannot appear relaxed if your voice is high and shrill.

Variation

A good speaker will vary the pitch and tone of his voice according to the message or point of emphasis. He will speak with a normal low tone, but can raise the pitch to punctuate a thought, or do voice characterizations. Technically, the term "monotonous" means "same pitch" (mono = one, tone). No speaker can hold an audience long if he speaks with a monotone. Keep your speech alive by changing the pitch, force, volume, rate of speaking, and voice quality.

One of the most effective means of achieving flexibility and variety is to practice different moods with a word or a sound. With "oh" or "ah", express the following:

(1) sudden pain
(2) exhaustion
(3) fright
(4) sarcasm
(5) pleasant surprise
(6) good natured sympathy
(7) hesitation
(8) indignation.

Also read aloud and watch out for expression. Be sure to read poetry often.

Exercises: Read a poem or the lyrics to a great hymn to the class. Tell a children's story, using dialogue and voice characterizations for a story such as three little pigs.

(Since this is homiletics, see if you can include the Biblical character analogies that are clearly illustrated.[3]

Use vocal techniques appropriate to the character and thought being communicated.

Speaking with Grace

"Let your speech be always with grace, seasonsed with salt, that ye may know how ye ought to answer every man." [4]

The Greek word for grace is *"charis,"* which is related to *"charisma,"* or gift. In our western culture, we think of a gift as something we get for nothing, hence the shallow definition, "unmerited favor." But biblical grace is much more than that. When God gives spiritual gifts, He holds us accountable for them. He is still the owner, and we are responsible to use them for others. Grace is better defined as the spiritual impartation of divine aptitudes and abilities: the "enablements" which we receive from the Holy Spirit apart from our human personality or achievement. Therefore, to "speak with grace" is to speak with spiritual anointing and inspiration, as well as to speak with compassion and deference to the needs of people. We should speak with a passion to encourage and edify people, rather than using speech to manipulate or to exalt ourselves over others.

Graceful speech is never cold, mechanically affected, or based on calculated tricks. Our motive in preaching should never be to control people or to get their money. We should always be motivated by a passionate love for God, which naturally flows to a love and compassion for people.

"We are not out to exercise dominion over your faith.
We want to be helpers of your joy." [5]

---

[3] I Corinthians 3:12-13
[4] Colossians 4:6
[5] II Corinthians 1:24

Our speech should also be "seasoned with salt." In the Bible, salt is related to covenant. It is valuable as a preservative. Salty speech is therefore kind, and based on preserving relationships, as opposed to harsh divisive speaking to lord over others.

Do Not Shout!

Lyman Beecher said, "the shouter is a speaker who has nothing much to say". He attempts to make up for lack of content by sheer vocal volume. This kind of speaking conceals nothing. It never works effectively, and listeners resent being overwhelmed by a rush of sound.

Just as excessive volume in a music recording is intolerable and oppressive, so excessive loudness in speech drowns out the over-tones and inflections which make it a living instrument.

Speak with feeling.

Good talkers feel before they speak. As one old southern preacher said years ago, "We don't go on feelings. But praise God we can feel what we're goin' on." To be "spiritual" does not mean that we eliminate our intellect or emotion. It simply means that the spirit is the dominant drive in our life. But when we are spiritual, our whole being is positively affected. We will think, feel, and exercise our will. Our spirit does not come alive to the exclusion of our soul. In fact, we should be even more sensitive in our soul.

"Eloquent speech is not from lip to ear, but rather from
heart to heart."
W. J. Bryan.

Emotion warms the voice only when it is controlled. The shout of anger, the cry of hate, the rantings of an Adolph Hitler is emotion mastering instead of mastered. We also have a natural tendency to communicate feelings, both positive and negative, so we need to be sure our attitudes are right before we start speaking.

Be sincere.

Some of the things which may be interpreted as insincerity are: excessive cuteness, false modesty ("I'm a poor speaker"), assumed convictions, meticulous uttering of every syllable to demonstrate speech superiority.

The word "sincere" comes from the Latin, "sin-cere (without wax)." In ancient Rome, wax was often used by vendors to cover cracks in marble pieces, or in pottery. When the piece was put under pressure or fire, it would then break. Potters and stone-cutters began advertising "sin-cere" products, meaning that there were no weaknesses that were covered up with wax. To be sincere means to be honest and genuine, with no hidden motives.

Be Simple and Clear.

Simple, heart-warming words in everyday speech tends to communicate sincerity and honesty. We tend to come across as pretentious when we talk over people's heads. Whether in speech or writing, clarity is necessary if you are to put your ideas across. Remember that the average preacher has a much larger vocabulary than the average listener. Our purpose is not to impress people with our level of literacy, but to communicate the message of the gospel. Put another way, your objective should not be to lead people to see how great you are, but to see how great God is.

The Apostle Paul learned that lesson in his ministry. He engaged in a brilliant intellectual debate in the city of Athens on Mars Hill. This was the seat of the humanistic Greek culture, where the intellectuals of the day met to impress themselves with their logic and wit. Paul, who could speak twenty-seven languages and was perhaps the most thoroughly educated man of his generation, delivered a powerful message about the "unknown god" to the humanists. He won every argument. He was profound and logical, but he failed to win any converts. His conclusion:

> *"I determined not to know anything among you, save Jesus Christ, and him crucified."* [6]

To these same Corinthian Christians, he later said,
> *"I fear, lest by an any means, as the serpent beguiled Eve through his subtility, so your minds should be corrupted from the simplicity that is in Christ."* [7]

Be enthusiastic.

Life attracts life. Animation reveals that we are sensitive to the feelings, hopes, and aspirations of those about us. The word "enthuse" comes from the Greek "Theo," which is a reference to "God." To be genuinely "enthused," you would have to have something from God in you. Jeremiah had a prophetic word from God "like fire, shut up in my bones. I have to speak it!" Now that, properly defined, is enthusiasm, as opposed to self-centered human energy expended on silly ball games.

Stock up with human interest stories

Not all these stories need be humorous, but they should all be relevant to the central topic. Some preachers are noted for starting

---

[6] I Corinthians 2:2

[7] II Corinthians 11:3

every sermon with a joke, or funny story to "break the ice" and warm up to the congregation. This is permissible, since it has a defined purpose. But it is better to share something interesting or funny in the context of the message to illustrate a central thought being communicated. Some of the most interesting speakers are students of history. They can make a truth come alive by sharing something from the life of an historical figure, and telling the story with a colorful word picture.

Help others unselfishly.

To be interesting, be interested. It is a basic law of self-expression. Someone once said, "I don't care how much you know until I know how much you care." If your central focus is on being accepted, liked, or successful as a speaker, you will tend to lose the audience to some degree. People pick up on that, and react to it.

Jesus was so popular because He was so compassionate about people. He never used people selfishly. Everything He did was giving, either to the Father, or to people. He saw Himself as a servant, with no rights or demands on the people. People responed to that by the thousands. Children were drawn to Him, because He had such a quick, genuine smile, and an obvious heart of love. The flocked around Him, because He was not out to make a great sermon, but to meet the needs of people.

Use the Voice Effectively

Phrase, Pause, and Stress.

Reading aloud is an effective way of learning.
It doubles the sense impressions and makes eye and ear more discriminating.

Secure and maintain a sense of communication.

It is not enough to read. You should read to somebody. Unless you are able to get the attention and interest of listeners, you cannot entertain, influence, or inform them.

To get the attention of listeners:

- Look them in the eyes.
- Project your voice "to the listener".
- Speak with vigor and expressiveness. A monotonous speaker quickly loses his audience.
- Study your material so carefully that you understand it and can put it into your own words.
- Learn the correct pronunciation of the words you are using.
- Learn the definition of any word with which you are not familiar.
- Use voice characterizations when appropriate.
- Maintain some level of eye contact, whenever possible. This is done by reading ahead, and knowing where you are on the page.

Get in the proper mood.

- The reader as speaker must be emotionally sensitive to what he reads in order to transmit the emotion to his hearers.
- A good reader involves himself in the selection. Never force your feelings into a part. Let it take hold of you.
- Relax, and get in an appropriate mood.
- Avoid being too obvious or excessive with emotions. They should be suggested.
- Be casual; do not over-emotionalize.

Pause wisely.

The pause is potentially one of the most useful instruments of vocal expression.

In order to appear conversational, pauses are an asset. The important thing is that you pause at the end of a phrase or thought. If you pause otherwise, you will appear to be, um, unsure of yourself. The only difference in appearance between a pause and a hesitation is the timing. A pause is deliberate, and comes across that way.

A pause does the following:
- It helps the speaker or reader to convey unexpressed feelings.
- It insinuates feelings.
- It arouses interest.
- It creates suspense.
- It stresses thoughts and mark transitions.
- It enables the speaker to breathe and retain his poise.
- It gives hearers a chance to absorb what they hear.

Group Words Properly.

The idea, and not the individual word, is the unit of thought. Grouping words in terms of ideas is technically called "phrasing". A phrase in speech is exactly like a phrase in music. It causes the theme to be expressed through a cohesive flow of words to communicate an idea or visual image.

Phrasing makes it possible to maintain the rhythmical flow of the sentence. When words are grouped in units that are too small, the resultant speech is choppy and coarse. When they are placed in units that are too large (wordy), the result is confusion or boredom.

Emphasize Properly.

Reading should never be perfunctory. It should be a dynamic creative interpretation of material. Correct emphasis not only makes us understood, it also makes us effective.

Some ways to emphasize a Point:

- ☐ Pausing before or after an important word or phrase.
- ☐ Looking for key words and stressing them.

- ☐ Changing the pitch of one's voice (such as, applying force after quietness and quietness after force) quickly catches the attention of the listeners.
- ☐ Deliberate misquotation.
  - As, *"And be ye transformed by the removal of your minds..."* [8] Pause, and let them make the correction in their minds.
- ☐ Appropriate humor (related to the topic)
- ☐ Asking the listeners to verbalize an important phrase.
- ☐ A strong Appropriate gesture or movement.

Speak or read loudly enough for all to hear.

If you read with a soft wimpy voice, people will have a difficult time understanding you. On the other hand, if you are too loud for the room or audience, the people will be repelled, irritated, or weary of you.

Vary your rate

If you speak too rapidly, you will be irritating to the hearers, and will lose details in communicating. If you are reading too slowly, you will lose their interest. Of course, a phrase can become more effective if it is done at a distinctive rate, such as a humorous quotation or phrase in a rapid-fire mode, or elongated for emphasis. Just as the same volume level is monotonous, so also is the same rate of speech. Variety helps to maintain interest, especially when the phrases are varied appropriately to the topic.

There are several ways of changing pace in reading:

- Pauses may be lengthened.
- Words may be stretched: such as "the Amalekite must die e e e e."
- Speak in a fuller, richer tone when you come to important words.

---

[8] Romans 12:2 Reversed Standard Version

Use correct inflections

Speech monotony is frequently caused by failure in inflection. There are bends in the vocal pitch upward and downward.

The difference between singing and speaking is that singers express lyrics (words) with a defined series of sustained pitches and a structured rhythm. Speakers use pitch and rhythm, but it is spontaneous, are rarely sustained. Speakers also do not usually employ as much range to the tones used.

Three kinds of inflections

- The rising inflection expresses astonishment, doubt, uncertainty, inquiry, or hesitation.
- The falling inflection expresses a simple and direct statement, a command, or a conviction. It can also create a sense of finality when used with interrogative pronouns such as who, which, why, how, and what.
- The circumflex or wavering inflection indicates a double meaning such as sarcasm, satire, insincerity, or curiosity.

Chapter Two

The Formal Platform Speech

First Step: "Ho Hum!"

In the first section of your speech, start a fire!

You must kindle a quick flame of interest in your first sentence. When you speak, do not picture your audience as waiting with eager eyes and baited breath to catch your message.

Picture your audience as looking uneasily at their watches, stifling yawns and saying, "Ho hum". The first sentence of your speech must crash through your audience's initial apathy. For example, do not open a speech on "safety first" by saying, "The subject assigned to me is 'the reduction of traffic accidents.'" Instead, try something like, "Four hundred and fifty shiny new coffins were delivered to the city last Thursday."

Once a famous preacher named Henry Ward Beecher went to a town called "Death Valley" because the preacher there was not getting the attention of his congregation. He strode to the front of the platform, wiping his brow, and said "It's a Goddam hot day." People almost fell from their seats. He paused and went on. "That's what I heard a man say this afternoon." Then he went on and preached a stirring sermon against blasphemy, with the full attention of the audience.

Second Step: "Why Bring That Up?"

At this point you need to build a bridge. Your listener lives on an island of his own interests. Why should he worry about what you have to speak about? This section of your speech must answer the question, "why bring this subject up?". For example: If you are talking about a jungle war in Bolivia, people will generally be mentally detached until you connect it to something they are interested in; such as the price of coffee and the other Bolivian exports.

Once, a doctor was speaking to a P.T.A. group on the grave topic of insanity. The parents were not interested until he said, "Your child today has almost one chance in twenty of being in an asylum before he dies." It makes no difference whether the subject of your speech is jungle warfare or insanity. You must build a bridge to your listeners.

Third Step: "For Instance!"

Get Down to Cases.

The body of your sermon must be keyed to one demand -- "for instance". If you start your message by asserting that "pride goes before destruction", then let your next sentence be "for instance, Herod gave a great speech. When he received the praise and worship of the people, he was eaten by worms. As he lay dying, with worms crawling in and out of his mouth and various other body parts, he probably experienced some level of humility before he assumed room temperature."

Another illustration illustrates the statement: "God honors faith." For instance, look at Hebrews chapter eleven, which is God's "Hall of Fame". If you read Proverbs 26:27 ("Whoso diggeth a pit shall fall into it."), then you can illustrate it with the story of Haman in the book of Esther as your "for instance".

Never present your "for instances" in a jigsaw jumble. Present them as organized platoons - in marching order. When one platoon marches by, that should be the end of it. Do not go back and say, "Oh, by the way - while I was on the subject of pride I should have mentioned..." It is generally more effective to omit a good illustration than to appear confused and poorly prepared.

Listeners appreciate speakers who serve their "for instances" as course dinners, not goulash. Illustrations must be clearly coordinated with the points to which they directly relate. The anecdotes, stories, and analogies are the "meat" on the bones (outline). To be useful, they must be rightly connected, or the body cannot function efficiently.

Generally, the most interesting and life-changing illustrations are true stories. People still love to hear biographies, even if they are no longer kids. They gain more from truths that are shown to be practical realities in lives and in history. Fiction is easier to develop because you do not need to have accurate dates, spelling, and other data, but it is worth the effort to study history and use true illustrations.

Fourth Step: So What?

In Conclusion. -- Ask the listeners for specific action.

The end of your sermon is like a pencil. It is much more useful if it has a point. It must be more than a graceful leave-taking. It must be more than a review of the "for instances". It must be more than a reminder of your subject's general importance. It must answer the question, "So what?"

In the conclusion, you are bringing the message to their doorstep. You have presented a truth from God's Word, and you want them to do something with it. In Acts 2, Peter stood with the eleven apostles and preached a great sermon. Some suggest that it was very short, but note that verse 40 says *"and with many other words did he testify and exhort."* It was a long sermon, involving both testimonies (examples) and exhortations. The people cried out, *"What shall we do?"* Peter had a ready answer. *"Repent, and be baptized every one of you."* From the time Peter began to speak, he had that goal in mind. He exalted the Jesus they had just crucified. He was leading them to the conclusion that they needed to repent of their sins, and make a covenant with God through Jesus Christ. He knew exactly what he wanted them to do.

You must have a purpose in speaking, other than to impress people or earn your honorarium. If you are preaching to unsaved people, you will always want them to repent and believe on the Lord Jesus Christ. If you are preaching to believers, then you want to exhort and inspire them to pray, or to give, or to teach them to forgive, or to train them to serve God in specific ways. You must lead them somewhere, and you must have something you want them to do differently.

"To talk much and arrive nowhere is the same as climbing a tree to catch a fish."

I think the pastor has been studying
the biography of Billy Graham.

SPEECH SUBSTANCE

Listeners' Laws for Speech Substance

In the preceding section you learned a two-word formula for investing the body of a speech. This formula applies to any and all speeches. Of course, you cannot apply this formula without preparation. If you run out of "for instances" the body of your speech has come to an end. No amount of speech organization can make up for lack of speech substance. No amount of manner can make up for insufficient matter. You cannot give "for instances" until you have prepared them to give.

Six "for instances" that listeners like best:

1. In story form.

This is in great demand. Generally, the most popular and effective preachers today are good storytellers. They are able to do more than just convey an idea. They can paint pictures in the minds of listeners with words. It is fast becoming a lost art in the age of technical visual communications, but it is still a wonderful skill.

Illustration:
A small boy was walking with his father one day, enjoying the beauty of the open field. He looked up and said, "Papa, how could it be that Jesus could die for the sins of the whole wide world? He was only one man." The wise father replied, "Son, do you see that wheel barrel? What if it was full of worms? Would you be more valuable to me than all of them?"
"Yes, Papa."
"Now, do you see that mountain over there? What if it was a great mountain of worms? Would you still be more valuable to me than all of them?"
"Oh, yes Papa!" And then he understood.

"Alas, and did my Savior bleed, and did my Sovereign die.

Would He devote that sacred head for such a worm as I?"

2. For instances that involve famous people

Even the story about the little boy was interesting; it would be more interesting if it were about George Washington, Thomas Edison, or someone famous.

Illustration:
About twenty years before America's Revolutionary War, George Washington was serving as an officer in the French and Indian War. He was only twenty-three years old, but he was tall, strong, and highly intelligent. The Americans fought with the British against the French. Colonel Washington was leading thirteen hundred troops from the Virginia militia against a French fort. On the way, they were ambushed in a ravine by a large group of French and Indian fighters. The British were vulnerable targets in the open area, while the Frenchmen and Indians were shooting from behind trees and trenches on the sides. After two hours of carnage, more than seven hundred British soldiers lay dead. Washington was the only officer left alive and on a horse. When he later took off his coat, he found four bullet holes in it. He said, "God protected me."

Fifteen years later, he went back to the Pennsylvania woods where the battle occurred. An old Indian chief heard that he was coming, and traveled many miles to meet him. He said, "You don't know me, but I was a chief in that battle. I ordered my men to shoot at you, because you were obviously the leader, and we would route the soldiers. I personally fired seventeen rounds at you at close range. I have traveled all this way to see the man that God would not let me kill."

3. For instances that animate the pages of history

If your story form "for instance" dramatizes an incident in recorded history it carries persuasive weight.

Illustration:
In 1588, King Phillip II of Spain decided to conquer England. He had the world's most powerful navy. The "Spanish Armada"

sent to conquer the British Isles consisted of one hundred and thirty ships, and involved thirty thousand men. When Queen Elizabeth heard of the coming invasion, she went to the sea port and personally led a time of prayer and fasting. A crowd gathered to cry out to God, as the little English fleet set out to protect its land.

When they engaged the Spaniards, a strong wind came up behind them, enabling the British to fire cannons at long range. At night, they set fire ships into the Spanish fleet, using the good wind again to their advantage. In a subsequent sea battle, the Spaniards decided to retreat, and the wind shifted in just the right direction. As they sailed around Scotland, a terrible storm arose, sinking many of their ships. Less than half of the world's greatest fleet made it home.

(By the way, most of our modern history textbooks omit any reference to the great British prayer meeting.)

4. Listeners like "for instances" based on colorful analogies.

Analogies as a rule are your most effective weapons of exposition.

Graft the new idea your listeners might have difficulty in understanding into an old idea which they do understand.

Illustration:

Jesus Christ was a master at using analogies. When He spoke to farmers, He said,

> 3 *"Behold, a sower went forth to sow;*
> 4 *And when he sowed, some {seeds} fell by the way side, and the fowls came and devoured them up:*
> 5 *Some fell upon stony places, where they had not much earth: and forthwith they sprung up, because they had no deepness of earth:*
> 6 *And when the sun was up, they were scorched; and because they had no root, they withered away.*

> 7 And some fell among thorns; and the thorns sprung up, and choked them:
> 8 But other fell into good ground, and brought forth fruit, some an hundredfold, some sixtyfold, some thirtyfold. [9]

Jesus used many analogies. An analogy is drawing a comparison between two things that are not related, such as "the kingdom of heaven is like a man searching for treasure..." Psalm 23 is an analogy, as is Matthew 13. When speaking to fishermen, Jesus used the fish to teach them about evangelism. Most of the parables of Jesus were based on analogies. It is said that one of the evidences of mature intelligence is the ability to think in analogies.

5. "For Instances" which dramatize important statistics.

"Sex education in America is counterproductive!" So exclaims a speaker. What is the quickest way to prove such a statement? By analogy stories, or by animating past history? No. You must give statistics. Listeners are persuaded by specific numbers if they are really important, easy to understand, and properly dramatized.

"After sex education was introduced in the state of California, official state records showed that the incidents of pregnancies and venereal diseases increased by more than 400% in the first ten years."

"For Instances" interwoven with visual aids.

The eyes of the audience tend to retain more information than the ears. Appeal to them as often as possible. It has been said that, on average, we remember less than 10% of what we hear, 20% of what we see, but 50% of what we both see and hear.

Chalkboards or overhead projectors are excellent tools when they are available. Some teachers will paint a picture (usually a landscape) with pastel chalk or paints. If you are speaking about the "sword of the Spirit," try to get a sword to hold in your hand,

---

[9] Matthew 13:3-8

and use it for gestures. If it's a real sword, you might even use it when you take up an offering.

"The light of the body is the eye: if therefore thine eye be single, thy whole body shall be full of light." [10]

Informal Conference Room Speech

Two Requirements:

The lively interaction of many minds.

The ideal number of people in the informal conference setting is between ten and twenty participants. The advantage is that the speaker can get immediate feedback and input, beyond the facial expressions and body language they get when delivering a monologue speech. A good discussion moderator will communicate his ideas while involving other people in a controlled discussion. He will get fresh insights from the others, and often some vivid illustrations from their experiences. The leader must try to draw out the shy ones, and keep the "talkaholic" from

---

[10] Matthew 6:22

monopolizing the time. If done tactfully and skillfully, the audience can be made to feel like a vital part of the meeting, rather than a spectator.

An exact issue under discussion.

As in all public speaking, there must be a definite purpose and goal. It is easy for a conference room speech to dissolve into a parlor room chat, or even into a verbal brawl, if the leader is not effective in steering the conversation down a defined course.

Five Rules:

- Speak to only reason for or against the idea being presented at a given time.
- Condensing an idea into one unforgettable sentence is far better than a lengthy monologue.
- Use your key issue sentence at the beginning of the meeting.
- Support your key issue sentence with "for instances".
- Repeat your key issue sentence as your closing sentence.

The Speech of Introduction

Laws to Remember:

- You must be brief.
- Avoid stale and stilted phrases.
- Do not embarrass the speaker.
- Do not exaggerate.
- Do not give the speaker false starts.
- Do not steal the spotlight.

Four simple audience questions to be answered:

1. Why this subject? (The world at this hour is open for the Gospel).
2. Why before this audience? (You as Christians have a mandate from the Lord in the Great Commission).
3. Why at this time? (The time is short).
4. Why by this speaker?
("This man has ministered the gospel in sixty nations around the world. I present now -- Dr. Smith.")

The story has often been repeated in Toastmasters Clubs about the embarrassing example of what not to do from the Depression-era. A man was told that he would have the honor of introducing the wife of the President of the United States, Eleanor Roosevelt, at a formal banquet. He was thrilled, but awed by the prospect of such an honor. Hoping to get everything just right, he went to seek the advice of a famed speaker in the city. The man said, "Well, the general rule of introduction is that the more famous the personality, the less information is really needed. If you are introducing Mrs. Roosevelt, I would suggest "the shorter the better." The man thanked him for his advice, and memorized his introduction. He went to the banquet, and stood to introduce the speaker. "Ladies and gentlemen, it is my good pleasure to introduce Mrs. Eleanor Roosevelt, and the less said the better."

The After-Dinner Speech

The most appropriate time to use humor is the after-dinner speech. In Christian circles, this usually involves a specific holiday or social occasion, such as a "Sweetheart Banquet" for couples, or Christmas party. While we always avoid anything suggestive or off-color, we should be able to generate laughter from our audience. This is not a time to stir people up about the end of the world. It is generally a time to share with one another around a table: to create happy memories.

Of course, we should never make humor at the expense of each other. Generally, we should demonstrate a willingness to laugh at ourselves: to get people to laugh with us.

A Few Pointer Regarding Humorous Speaking

- Humorous stories should be used to illustrate specific points, rather than just for the sake of eliciting a laugh.
  However, this general rule is somewhat relaxed in the after-dinner setting, particularly if the dinner is a social or entertaining gathering.
- Make the transition casual, not too obvious.
- Make transitions purposeful.
- Avoid using puns.
- Avoid cliches like the plague.
- Be able to tell the story well.

No, Johnson. The Bible says that God chose the foolishness of preaching; not foolish preaching.

Listener's Laws for Speech Phraseology

Listeners like speech phraseology that is "free from wax".

Superlatives:	"the finest... brightest....happiest...." "more than the greatest love the world has known...."
Trite:	"You may be lost and undone."
Jargon:	"You need to come to the cross, lay your sins at the feet of Jesus, and be redeemed by the precious blood of the Lamb."
Groping:	"and...uh...well... somebody say amen...."
Repetitious:	"somebody else say amen…"
Weasel words:	"As I said before", "it's only my opinion".
Creating mental images:	Be careful that you do not say something that will cause the listeners to visualize something inappropriate. One preacher, after reading his initial Bible text, said, "And now my co-text is..."

Listeners like speech phraseology that is grammatically correct.

Poor grammar will diminish the confidence of the listener in the speaker, even if the ideas are Biblical and well thought out.
"I cease to be amazed..."
"I could care less."
"That would work for him and I."

Listeners like speech phraseology with good "connective tissue"

(connecting words): "consequently", "therefore", "as a result", "notwithstanding".

Listeners like speech phraseology that is conversational.

The best speakers tend to make the listeners feel as if they are listening to a friend talking with them personally, rather than an orator who is directing a crowd. Speaking in low, clear tones, using eye contact, smiling, and using personal illustrations help make the speaker more conversational. The opposite would be to sound confrontational, or mechanical.

Listeners like speech phraseology that is specific.

Try not to say, "a couple of trees". Instead, say, "a maple and a black walnut tree".
At the wedding of Cana of Galilee, they did not just have some water. They had six stone water pots which the Jews used for purification. They each held two or three firkins of water. Jesus did not just turn all of the water into wine. He turned it into very good wine.

Listeners like speech phraseology that is picturesque

Name specific things. Rather than saying, "They went for a walk," say, "They were strolling down the narrow, dusty road, hardly noticing the mighty oak trees which shaded them intermittently."

Listeners like speech phraseology that is clear.

If you can communicate your thought clearly, you will tend to be more convincing.

Listener's Laws for Speech Delivery

Pleasing his Eyes.

- Look at the people to whom you are speaking.
- Look at all your listeners. Try not to focus on one or two people.
  (However, you may find it helpful to focus more on a few who are responsive and positive, and not on someone who is glaring or looking antagonistic.)
- Actually see your listeners. Do not focus on your notes, or on the back wall.
- Maintain an alert body carriage.
- Make your body behave.
- Gesture; do not gestulate.
  Gestures are controlled and defined. They seek to illustrate the point as much as possible. They are carefully coordinated with the word being spoken, and are not overdone.

Pleasing his Ears.

- Talk! Remember that you are not there just to make an oration.
- Talk with animation, appropriately varying vocal pitch, adequate volume, and at the right rate of speed.
- Talk clearly. Enunciate words so that every phrase can be easily understood.
- Talk with composure.
- Pauses should punctuate rather than mutilate the phrases.
- Pause clearly. A pause done inappropriately or excessively will come across as hesitation.

A well-rounded speaker should learn to do the following:

Introduction.
Welcome and greeting.
Response.
Presentation.
Acceptance.
Farewell.
Dedication.
Anniversary.
Eulogy.
After dinner.
Exposition.
Campaign.
Official duties.
Nomination.
Book review.
Radio.
Discussion meeting.

Suggested Projects

Practice giving speeches for the following:

A Wedding.

Just do the wedding sermon. If you follow the lead of Paul, you will find it to be an excellent analogy for our relationship with God.

(Ephesians 5)

A Funeral.

Give a message on the certainty and finality of death.
To take a lighter approach, give a proposed eulogy for yourself, or for a classmate.

A Gift Presentation.

Present a plaque or gift to the church, a class gift at graduation, a library or books to a school.

An After-Dinner Speech.

1. You are to address a business and professional men's dinner to organize Bible distribution in public schools.
2. You are the after-dinner speaker for your city's Christian business men and pastors. The banquet is being given to start a local "Youth for Christ" rally.
3. You are the motivational speaker for a P.T.A. dinner. The goal of the meeting is to curb crime in the local high school.
4. You are speaking at a dinner with district ministers for the purpose of arousing interest and support for Bible Institute.
5. You are speaking for a missions banquet to encourage people to give huge sums of money to the missionaries.

Other practice needed:

1. Memorize and recite a poem. It can be comical, inspirational, or informative.
2. Read a children's stories using several voice characterizations.
3. Tell an interesting story with the point of illustrating something difficult to understand. (analogy)
4. Give an object lesson in an effort to sell something or cause people to contribute to something.
5. Give a patriotic speech at some holiday celebration (with a spiritual lesson in it).
6. Express moods and feelings. Use the following sentences in many different shades of feeling.

    a. **"We will not be defeated."**
    b. **"The boat is sinking; what shall we do?"**
    c. **"The King is coming!"**
    d. **"I know exactly what I'm going to do."**

7. Repeat the last sentence several times, placing the voice accent on a different word each time. Note the change in the meaning.

The following outlines and quotations are based upon the book, "Public Speaking and Influencing Men in Business", written by Dale Carnagie. The purpose of this course is to help you to be better able to speak forth the unsearchable riches of Christ. We ask that you prayerfully and with determination approach this subject to be better equipped to serve in the Master's army.

Developing Courage and Self-Confidence.

Start with a strong desire

When Julius Caesar sailed over the channel from Gaul and landed with his legions on what is now England, what did he do to insure the success of his arms? A very clever thing: he halted his soldiers on the chalk cliffs of Dover, and looking down over the waves two hundred feet below, they saw the red tongues of fire consume every ship in which they had crossed. In the enemy's country, with the last link with the continent gone, there was but one thing left for them to do; to advance, to conquer. That is precisely what they did. Such was the spirit of the immortal Caesar. Why not make it yours too, in this war to exterminate your foolish fear of audiences.

Know thoroughly what you are going to talk about.

Unless a man has thought out and planned his talk and knows what he is going to say, he cannot feel very comfortable when he faces his auditors. He is like the blind leading the blind. A poorly prepared speaker tends to be self-conscious. In fact, he ought to feel repentant and ashamed of his negligence.

> "I was elected to the Legislature in the fall of 1881", Teddy Roosevelt wrote in his autobiography, "and found myself the youngest man in that body. Like all young men and inexperienced members, I had considerable difficulty in teaching myself to speak. I profited much by the advice of a hard-headed old countryman. The advice ran:

'Don't speak until you are sure you have something to say, and know just what it is; then say it, and sit down.'"

He ought to have added: "It will help you to throw off your embarrassment if you can find something to do before an audience -- if you can exhibit something, write a word on the blackboard, or point out a spot on the map, or move a table, or throw open a window, or shift some books and papers -- any physical action with a purpose behind it may help you to feel more at home." True, it is not always easy to find an excuse for doing such things, but there is the suggestion. Use it if you can, but use it only the first few times. A baby does not cling to chairs after it once learns to walk.

Act Confident.

In every age, man has always admired courage. So, no matter how your heart may be pounding inside, stride forth bravely, stop, stand still, look your audience straight in the eyes like a conqueror, take a deep breath and speak. "In war", said Marshal Foch, "the best defensive is an offensive". So take the offensive against your fears. Go out to meet them, battle them, conquer them by sheer boldness at every opportunity. Have a message and then think of yourself as a telegram messenger instructed to deliver it. We pay little attention to the messenger. The message; that is the thing. Keep your mind on it. Keep your heart in it. Know it like the back of your hand. Then talk as if you were determined to say it.

Practice! Practice! Practice!

"Any beginner", warned Roosevelt, "is apt to have 'buck fever'". Buck fever means a state of intense nervous excitement that may be entirely separate from timidity. It may affect a man the first time he has to speak to a large audience just as it may affect him the first time he sees a buck or goes into battle. What such a man needs is not courage, but nerve control, cool headedness. This he can only get by actual practice. He must, by custom and repeated exercise of self-mastery, get his nerves thoroughly under control. This is largely a matter of habit. Any man will grow stronger and stronger with each exercise.

Self-Confidence through Preparation.

How can we ever hope to subdue the cohorts of fear when we go into the battle with wet powder and blank shells, or with no ammunition at all? "I believe", said Abraham Lincoln in the White House, "that I shall never be old enough to speak without embarrassment when I have nothing to say." A well-prepared speech is already nine-tenths delivered.

The Right Way to Prepare.

Let us cite an illustration of how to do it and how not to do it. A gentleman, whom we shall call Mr. Flynn, was a student of this course in Washington, D.C. One afternoon, he devoted his talk to eulogizing the capital city of the nation. He had hastily gleaned his facts from a booklet issued by a newspaper. They sounded like it; dry, disconnected, and undigested. He had not thought over his subject adequately. The whole affair was flat, flavorless and unprofitable.

A Speech that Cannot Fail.

A fortnight later, something happened that touched Mr. Flynn to the core: a thief stole his Cadillac out of a public garage. He rushed to the police and offered rewards, but it was all in vain. The police admitted that it was nearly impossible for them to cope with the crime situation; yet, only a week previously they had found time to walk about the street, chalk in hand, and fine Mr. Flynn because he had parked his car fifteen minutes overtime. These "chalk cops" who were so busy annoying respectable citizens that they could not catch criminals, aroused his ire. He was indignant. He had something to say, not something that he had gotten out of a book. It leaped out of his own experience. Now he had but to stand on his feet and open his mouth, and his condemnation of the police welled up and boiled forth like Mt. Vesuvius (active volcano) in action. A speech like that is almost foolproof.

Defining Preparation.

Real preparation consists in digging something out of yourself, as well as out of the Bible and related sources. Preparation also means assembling and arranging your thoughts in a systematic and cohesive order, and in knowing precisely what your convictions are on the matter at hand.

In preparing a sermon, the first order is prayer, and the second is the direct study of the Bible. You want a fresh inspiration from the Holy Spirit, but it must also be consistent with the Bible. Also, you usually should make notes, even if you do not need them in hand when you preach. An outline gives structure, while clear illustrations bring it life and flavor.

Remember:

Always keep in mind that the highest goal of preaching is to articulate what God is saying, rather than your own opinions. We cannot help but insert our own ideas into our discourse, but we want to keep it pure through prayer and a thorough knowledge of the text and context.

How Famous Speakers Prepared their Addresses.

A government official spoke at a luncheon, and this is the opinion of one of his listeners.

"His mind was, in short, a mere hodgepodge, and so was the mental feast he served us. He brought on the ice-cream first, and then placed the soup before us. Fish and nuts came next. And, on top of that, there was something that seemed to be a mixture of soup and ice-cream and good red herring. I have never, anywhere or at any time, seen a speaker more utterly confused. He knew his subject thoroughly but had not planned his speech. A speech is a voyage with a purpose, and it must be charted. The man who starts nowhere usually gets there. Put Napoleon's statement in your mind in bold letters, "THE ART OF WAR IS A SCIENCE IN WHICH NOTHING SUCCEEDS WHICH HAS NOT BEEN CALCULATED AND THOUGHT OUT." This is just as true of public speaking.

Some ways of planning a speech:

- State your facts. (Show something that is wrong).
- Argue from them. (Show how to remedy it).
- Appeal for Action. (Ask for cooperation).

Woodrow Wilson, Theodore Roosevelt, and Sir Oliver Lodge made skeleton notes and then added meat to the "bones" by additional notes. Only then did they dictated and write their speeches. Most speakers will agree that using notes while speaking tends to diminish the effectiveness of the message, both because of the loss of eye contact, and because the speaker appears less familiar with his material. If notes must be used, make them as brief as possible. Do not memorize your talk word by word. Study the careers of famous speakers and you will find one fact that is true of all of them: they **PRACTICED**.

The Improvement of Memory

"The average man", said Professor Carl Seashore, "does not use above ten percent of his inherited capacity for memory. He wastes the ninety percent by violating the natural laws of remembering". These "natural laws of remembering" are:

impression, repetition, and association.

Impression

Get a vivid impression of the thing that you want to remember. To do that you must: concentrate, observe closely, use as many senses as possible, and above all, get an eye impression

Repetition

Here are a few hints to make repetition fruitful. Do not sit down and repeat a thing over and over until you have memorized it. Go over it once or twice and then drop it. Come back later and go over it again. After we have memorized something, we forget as much during the first eight hours as we do during the next thirty days. So, go over your notes just a few minutes before you rise to make your talk.

Association

The only way that we can remember is to associate one thing with another thing. This will form a joint picture that will remain. To remember the points of your address, arrange them in logical order. A nonsense sentence may help. If you do forget your point, use the last word of your previous sentence to form a new sentence. Do this until point is remembered.

Keeping the Audience Awake

Be exciting by being excited.

"Every great movement in the annals of history", said Emerson, "is the triumph of enthusiasm". Passion, feeling, spirit, and enthusiasm are vital to an effective sermon. It is not enough to know what you are talking about. You must communicate a sense of knowing who you are talking about, and why it matters both to you and to your audience. If this is accomplished, your audience will overlook minor mistakes.

Make sure that you have something to say.

To achieve this, you may have to dig deep to form a conviction on a topic but by all means form it and speak it as though your life depended on your success. The secret of a triumph is that your subject takes a grip on you. Dwight L. Moody became so stirred in the preparation of his sermon on "Grace" that he seized his hat, left his study, strode out into the street, and accosted the first man he met with the abrupt inquiry: "Do you know what grace is?"

Act with sincere passion.

Acting in earnest makes one feel in earnest. Gesture! Above all, speak out so that everyone can hear you. A country preacher once asked Henry Ward Beecher how to keep an audience awake on a hot Sunday afternoon, and Beecher told him to have an usher take a sharp stick and prod the preacher. Use any means as shadow-boxing, running, swimming, frantic gestures, etc., to work up enthusiasm just before speaking. Leave out words like "it seems", "in my humble opinion", etc. Speak rather from a conviction of the **truth**. A real love for your audience will do wonders for your speech.

Be Persistent

This chapter can be stated in just a few sentences. Persistence is a must. Be mentally victorious and the physical will follow. General Foch's message should be our battle cry, "My center gives way. My right recedes. The situation is excellent. I shall attack". The attack saved Paris and an attack will save you from failing. DETERMINATION is ninety percent of accomplishment.

The Secret of Good Delivery.

"It is not so much what you say, but how you say it". Delivery is getting the message to the audience. Be natural in your speaking. Remember these important exhortations about delivery:

- Stress important words with inflection, gestures, and/or pauses.
- Change the pitch as well as the tone of your voice to create varying moods, or to emphasize different points.
- Vary your rate of speaking appropriately for the moment.
- Pause before and after important ideas. Be sure that you do not overdo a pause, or you will appear to be groping for the next thought.
- Make eye contact. Never stare at the ceiling or back walls when you are speaking.
- Speak as if you are addressing one person. The most effective speakers make the listeners feel as if he is speaking directly and personally to them.

Platform Presence.

This is one of the most important things in this course.

Watch closely the following:

- **Personality is a must.** Make sure you are rested, encouraged, and spiritually in tune.
- Eat sparingly before speaking. A heavy meal will tend to divert the circulatory system to the digestive track, and leave you less alert. Of course, it is not necessary to labor the obvious point about burping.
- Do nothing that might dull your energy.
- Dress neatly, and appropriately for the occasion. It is generally better to be a little overdressed than underdressed if you are the speaker. Your choice of clothing says much about your attitude toward the people to whom you are speaking.
- Smile much of the time. A frown tends to draw attention to self, and demand pity or attention. Smiles cause the people to relax and be more receptive.
- Crowd your audience together. If possible, meet in a room which is the right size for the group. A room that is too large causes people to think that "nobody showed up." On the other hand, a crowded room has much more exciting room dynamics, and has a positive psychological effect.
- If the group is small, avoid limiting yourself to the platform.
- Keep the air fresh.
- Flood the room with lights if possible.
- Do not stand behind furniture; and try not to be on the platform alone.
- Do not flop down in the chair.
- Stand still; let your hands fall easily at your side.
- Make sure your hand movements appear natural. Let your gesture continue until the climax of the point that you are trying to emphasize.

How to Open a Talk

Opening any speech is difficult, especially if you are addressing an audience which is not familiar with you. As a result, it should be carefully prepared. The introduction should be as brief as possible.

Two mistakes to avoid:

Do not start with an apologizing statement. This will usually diminish your credibility, and indicate an undue focus on self.

Do not start with a humorous story. Humor is usually good in sermons, and can be very effective when used to illustrate the sermon ideas. But humor for the sake of humor is generally distracting, and communicates the notion that you are there to make a good impression, rather than to make a positive difference in the lives of the people.

Immediate attention may be gained by:

- Arousing curiosity.
- Telling a human-interest story.
- Beginning with a specific illustration.
- Using an exhibit.
- Asking a question.
- Sharing a striking quotation.
- Revealing interesting and startling statistics.

Capture Your Audiences at Once.

To do this, you must begin on common ground. Do not state your case so that the audience says no. The best argument is that which seems merely an explanation. The most famous speech that Shakespeare ever wrote is Mark Anthony's funeral oration over

Caesar. He presents the facts, and lets them form their own opinions.

How to Close a Talk.

Many speakers make the common mistake of saying, "This is about all I have to say on the matter; so I guess I'll close". This kind of expression fails to make a conclusion. It is far better to leave the people with a sense of wanting more, or that you will have much more to say the next time you have the opportunity.

Some Options for Closing:

- Summarize and reiterate your main points.
- Make a compelling appeal for action.

  During the beginning of the American Revolution, one colonial pastor delivered a powerful message about the importance of freedom, and the Biblical basis for independence from the tyranny of the British throne. At the end of his message, he dramatically threw off his clerical robe to reveal his officer's army uniform, picked up his gun, and asked for men who would volunteer to fight with him. Now that was an altar call.

- Give a sincere compliment to the audience.

  "Bless your hearts, you folks have been so gracious and attentive through this long-winded sermon. Only three people fell asleep. Is this a great congregation or what?

- Make a humorous closing to leave them with a smile.

  "Well, I have just received a note here. It says, "Idiot!" Imagine that! I have received unsigned notes before, but this is the first time someone has signed one but forgot to write the message."

- Close with a poetic quotation that summarizes or reinforces the message.
- Recite a passage from the Bible which summarizes the theme of the message..

- Sing a verse of a song that relates directly to what you have just shared, or lead the people in singing it if it is familiar to most of them.

- The ending as well as the beginning should be carefully prepared. The opening and closing of a speech are the points where you can show your inexperience or your expertise.

Make Your Meaning Clear.

Do not leave your audience in a daze. Clarity can be attained by:

- Using comparisons.
- Avoiding technical terms.
- Knowing your subject thoroughly.
- Appealing to the sense of sight with visual aids.
- Restating your main ideas.
- Limiting yourself to one basic thought, with only a few supporting points.
- Closing with a brief summary of your points.

How to be Impressive and Convincing.

Our objective is to plant the idea in the minds of the listeners so that no contradictory and opposing ideas can arise. This can be achieved by the following:

1. Liken what you wish people to believe to something that they already believe.
2. Make small sums appear large and large sums appear small.
3. Make figures impressive by using word pictures.

4. Restate important points but do not repeat them with the identical wording.
5. Use general illustrations and specific instances.
6. Make sure all points strengthen the object of the sermon.
7. Quote known authorities to support your conclusion.
8. Be definite.
9. Quote a popular personality.
10. Quote local authorities.
11. Quote someone qualified to speak.
12. Quote the Bible as often as possible. Do not just read the texts.

Four basic ways by which we make impressions on other people:

- by what we do,
- by how we look,
- by what we say,
- by the way in which we say it.

Read only the best of books, such as the one your are reading now. Do not ignore the newspaper. Read it. Read with a dictionary by your side. Study the history of the words you use. Use synonyms freely to avoid repetition. Avoid using trite comparisons such as "cool as a cucumber". Strive for freshness.

Keep the People Interested

We are interested in extraordinary facts about ordinary things. Our chief interest is ourselves. Get others to talk about themselves to become a conversationalist. Glorified gossip, stories of people will always hold attention. Be concrete and definite. Sprinkle your talks with phrases that create pictures. Use balance sentences and contrasting ideas. Use descriptive terms that create vivid images in the mind. Stimulate the imagination. Interest is contagious.

Get Action.

This is the climax of your message. First, get the people's interest and attention. Secondly, win confidence by your sincerity, by being properly introduced, by being qualified to speak on your subject, and by telling the things that your experience has taught you. Third, state your facts clearly, concisely, and with verified sources. Fourth, appeal to the motives that make men act: the desire for gain, self-protection, pride, pleasures, sentiments, affections, and spiritual ideals, such as justice, mercy, forgiveness, and love.

In preaching, your goal is not just to stir the soul (mind, will, and emotion), but to touch the spirit (conscience, intuition, and communion). Your goal is to lead people to Biblical conclusions, such as loving, giving, serving, and consecration to God. Create a strong focus on God and His Word, and appeal to the conscience, as well as to the innate desire to know and understand God.

Part Two

Homiletics
The Art of Preaching

by Ken Chant
with Ernest Weaver

Chapter Three

The Preacher

The Importance of Preaching

"Preaching is the manifestation of the incarnate word, from the written word, by the spoken word."
Bernard Manning

"Therefore thus saith the LORD, If thou return, then will I bring thee again, and thou shalt stand before me: and if thou take forth the precious from the vile, thou shalt be as my mouth: let them return unto thee; but return not thou unto them." [11]

"And beginning at Moses and all the prophets, he expounded unto them in all the scriptures the things concerning himself." [12]

"For after that in the wisdom of God the world by wisdom knew not God, it pleased God by the foolishness of preaching to save them that believe." [13]

Note that Paul did not say, "foolish preaching." The great apostle took his preaching ministry very seriously, but he recognized that in the eyes of the world, the activity of preaching seems silly or absurd. Also, the divine purpose for preaching is not just to get people "born again." We equate salvation with regeneration, but it is a much broader term. The word *"sodzo"*

---

[11] Jeremiah 15:19
[12] Luke 24:27
[13] I Corinthians 1:21

means "to deliver, to heal, to make whole". God could speak directly to humanity, or He could use angelic messengers. Instead, God chooses to speak through ordinary people of His sovereign selection. He gives special abilities to those He ordains to be leaders, and they are responsible to serve as His messengers with a focus on His message and purpose in the earth.

> *"And all things are of God, who hath reconciled us to himself by Jesus Christ, and hath given to us the ministry of reconciliation;*
> *To wit, that God was in Christ, reconciling the world unto himself, not imputing their trespasses unto them; and hath committed unto us the word of reconciliation."* [14]

```
"Homiletics is the art and science of
              preaching".
  Homiletics deals with the preparation
          and the delivery of
        sermons and Bible lessons.
```

What is Preaching?

Preaching is the proclamation of the good news of salvation through man to men. Preaching involves a man and a message. Preaching presents the truth of the Bible through the personality of the preacher. Preaching is persuasive speaking with the declared purpose of turning the hearts of people to God. Good preaching always exalts and draws the most attention to Jesus Christ.

What is a Preacher?

A preacher is a person who is chosen and equipped by God for the specific work of the public declaration of the

---

[14] II Corinthians 5:18-19

truths of the Bible. He is called of God to teach, inspire, and encourage people from the Bible. He should always seek to speaks as "an oracle of God, " as opposed to spouting his own opinions.

> *"If any man speak, let him speak as the oracles of God; if any man minister, let him do it as of the ability which God giveth: that God in all things may be glorified through Jesus Christ, to whom be praise and dominion for ever and ever. Amen."* [15]

The word "oracle" means "mouthpiece." The highest level of preaching involves the greatest input from the Holy Spirit, with the least amount of resistance from the mind of the preacher. God will work through our personality and will draw from our research and knowledge, but His purpose is the speak through yielded vessels. The goal of a good preacher is "less of me, more of Him." Or, as John put it,

"He must increase, but I must decrease."

Obviously, the plumb line for truth is the Bible. We know that it is the proven Word of God. The goal of a good preacher is to hear from God, to know what Biblical message God has for the people he is addressing in this present situation. This requires spiritual sensitivity, and that requires prayer and humility.

The Personal Qualities of a Good Preacher.

A good preacher must not be an imitator of other men.

Have your own individuality. God made no two faces or voices alike. We have received the "manifold" grace of God. David killed his Goliath with the weapon he had grown up using. He was wise to refuse the armor of King Saul. We can all be tempted to see a successful ministry, and try to emulate the style.

---

[15] I Peter 4:11

But the essence of all successful ministry is prayer and hard work, not idiosyncratic style.

Seek to be the preacher that God has designed you to be. Be your best self. Be the anointed inspired vessel that God has designed you to be. Keep your focus on Jesus, and be like Him. We should, incidentally, be imitators of God.

> "Therefore, be imitators of God, as beloved children..." [16]

A good preacher must be a man of deep piety.

Piety is being dutiful toward God; of deep devotion and reverence to God. The preacher is short of power in the pulpit if his private life is not clean.
"Be ye clean, ye that bear the vessels of the Lord." [17]

A good preacher is a man who maintains clean habits.

He who sins secretly will be put to shame openly (Example: David). If his life is not clean and pure, he cannot face his people with confidence. Eventually, he will suffer for his moral failures. You cannot maintain a vibrant ministry with secret sin in your heart.

A good preacher must be a man of balance.

> We must be persuasive without being controlling.
> We must be exhorters without being manipulators.
> We must be loving without being lecherous.
> We must be humorous without being silly.
> We must be servants without being hirelings.
> We must be leaders without being tyrants.
> We must be equippers without being enablers.
> We must be sober without being boring.
> We must be simple without being condescending.
> We must be gentle without being wimps.

---

[16] Ephesians 5:1, NIV
[17] Isaiah 52:11

We must rebuke people without discouraging them.
We must encourage people without condoning sin.
We must pursue excellence without being perfectionists.

A good preacher must be truthful.

Exaggeration is lying. A lie in the pulpit is as bad as a lie elsewhere. In fact, it is worse, for it associates deception with the pulpit. How many preachers seek to impress others with inflated statistics about the breadth of their ministry. If we run 200 in Sunday School, and average 250 in the morning service, are we not tempted to say "we average 450 on Sunday mornings"? Many preachers add the attendance for all of their services, and let others think that it is the number for a single service. "Evangelastically speaking..."

If you are using an illustration that did not occur in your own life, then do not say that it did. We know it makes it more interesting if people visualize you doing it, but it is always better to be honest. If you have to make up stories about going out to witness because your own life is so barren, then perhaps you should go out and witness before you try to get such a reputation. Do not pretend to be in life what you are not in reality.

"Look, Paul. If you know I'm lying,
and I know you know I'm lying,
isn't that like telling the truth?"

A good preacher must be a man of gravity.

This does not mean "sour and mean." It means that the preacher is serious about life and eternity, considering whose servant he is and what court he represents. He can laugh and have a sense of humor, but he should not be given to foolish talking and jesting.

A good preacher should take care of his Physical Health.

You must be your best physically. We excuse our flabby bodies with the verse that says *"bodily exercise profiteth little."* Actually, that verse is better translated, *"bodily exercise hath a little profit."* Also, remember that Paul was speaking to people who walked everywhere they went, and were outdoors most of their waking hours. They did not sit at computers munching on Doritos all day long.

Some Basic Keys to Good Health

- ☐ Regular physical exercise. Get your heart beating fast for at least twenty minutes at least three times a week.
- ☐ A good diet, including fruits and vegetables, and high fiber foods. The average American eats an extremely high fat low-fiber diet, and we have the heart attacks to prove it. The staple of a diet in the Bible is bread. Today, the focal point of our meals is meat.
- ☐ Avoiding stress. You can avoid stress by regular prayer, a consistent daily schedule, and Biblical principles of resolving interpersonal conflicts. Also, praying in the Spirit is excellent for avoiding stress-related diseases.
- ☐ Drink more water, less coffee and soft drinks. The Mormons may be wrong on most of their doctrines, but they make a good point on caffeine and sugar.

> How many of us struggle with poor health, and die early, complaining that "I don't understand why God let this affliction come on me"?

Basic Requirements for Christian Ministry

The Call of God

> *"I have not sent these prophets, yet they ran: I have not spoken to them, yet they prophesied.*
> *But if they had stood in my counsel, and had caused my people to hear my words, then they should have turned them from their evil way, and from the evil of their doings."*[18]

---

[18] Jeremiah 23:21-22

"Some were called.
Some were sent.
Others just got up and went."

All believers are called to be "ministers." The word "minister" simply means "servant." We are all given spiritual gifts in order to help lead people to Jesus and disciple them to God. But some are "chosen," or set apart by God to be spiritual leaders in the church. This "call," or divine mandate, is not a reward for spiritual achievement, or an indication of superior intellect. It is simply the fact that God gives special grace for some to become preachers, and they will be held accountable to Him for they way they developed and used that grace.

> *"Therefore seeing we have this ministry, as we have received mercy, we faint not."* [19]

If you are not called by God to be a preacher, then do not become one, even if you inherit a fine church or your grandmother's dying wish was to have you in the ministry. If you can get out of it, then get out, and be a good businessman for God. But if you are called to preach, God will give you the ability to do it, and you will never be fulfilled in life pursuing another vocation or ministry. God will also open the right doors in His time. "We

---

[19] II Corinthians 4:1

are not responsible for the breadth of our ministry, only for the depth of our ministry." [20]

If you are called by God to preach, then you are responsible to know the Word of God, the Bible. You are also responsible to give yourself faithfully to prayer, so that you are hearing from God, and not just giving Bible book reports. If you are really called, you will know it, and the people to whom you preach will respond to it. If you are called to preach, you will have a deep need to do it, as Paul and Jeremiah did.

> *"For if I preach the gospel, I have nothing to glory of: for necessity is laid upon me; yea, woe is unto me, if I preach not the gospel!"* [21]

A Genuine Love for People

The Apostle Paul said to the Christians in Rome, "For I long to see you, that I might impart some spiritual gift, to the end that you may be established." [22] Jesus Himself said that love was the identifying quality for true disciples. [23] First Corinthians 13 begins with the concept that even great ministry, if it is not motivated by a love for people, is meaningless, and produces no reward.

Personal Qualities

Holiness

Personal holiness is not based on human effort, or "sweat" (Ezekiel 44:18 is an analogy about carnal efforts to be holy); but the dynamic holiness inwrought by the Holy Spirit. Something which is "sanctified" is set apart for a specific purpose. A sanctified vessel in the tabernacle was to be used for the sacrifices and the priesthood, and for nothing else. When our bodies are sanctified to God, then they are to be used for His glory and His

---

[20] Bill Gothard, Institute in Basic Life Principles, Lecture notes
[21] I Corinthians 9:16

[22] Romans 1:11
[23] John 13:35

work, and we do not have the right to use them for fornication or for selfish, wicked purposes. Holiness is not a set of rules and standards, but the moral result of a pure relationship with God. Holiness is not working for Jesus, but allowing Jesus to work through you.

The natural mind looks for qualities such as intelligence, strength, personality, and so on. But the nature is preaching is that of serving as a messenger, and character qualities far outweigh the importance of ability. When we preach, we are always tempted to receive the praises of people and take ourselves too seriously. Jeremiah put the values in place that we must always keep in mind.

> *"Thus saith the LORD, Let not the wise man glory in his wisdom, neither let the mighty man glory in his might, let not the rich man glory in his riches: But let him that glorieth glory in this, that he understandeth and knoweth me, that I am the LORD which exercise lovingkindness, judgment, and righteousness, in the earth: for in these things I delight, saith the LORD."* [24]

Sincerity

Thomas Carlyle, on Robert Burns (1759-96):

"The excellence of Burns is, indeed, among the rarest, whether in poetry or prose; but at the same time, it is plain and easily recognized: his sincerity, his indisputable air of Truth. Here are no fabulous joys or woes; no hollow fantastic sentimentalities; no wire drawn refinings, either in thought or feeling: the passion that is traced before us has glowed in a living heart; the opinion he utters has risen from his understanding, and been a light to his own steps. He does not write from hearsay, but from sight and experience; it is the scene that he has lived and labored amidst, that he describes: those scenes, rude and humble as they are, have kindled beautiful emotions in his soul, noble thoughts, and definite

---
[24] Jeremiah 9:24

resolves; and he speaks forth what is in him, not from any outward call of vanity or interest, but because his heart is too full to be silent. He speaks it with such melody and modulation as he can; "in homely rustic jingle"; but it is his own, and genuine. This is the grand secret for finding readers and retaining them: let him who would move and convince others, be first moved and convinced himself. Horace's rule, "Si vis me flere ..."[25] is applicable in a wider sense than the literal one. To every poet, to every writer, we might say: Be true, if you would be believed. Let a man but speak with genuine earnestness the thought, the emotion, the actual condition of his own heart, and other men - so strangely are we all knit together by the tie of sympathy - must and will give heed to him ... for in spite of all casual varieties in outward rank or inward, as face answers to face, so does the heart of man to man." [26]

Likewise this moving passage from Henry David Thoreau ...

"We talk of genius as if it were a mere knack, and the poet could only express what other men conceived. But in comparison with his task, the poet is the least talented of any; the writer of prose has more skill. See what talent the smith has. His material is pliant in his hands. When the poet is most inspired, is stimulated by an aura which never even colors the afternoons of common men, then his talent is all gone, and he is no longer a poet. The gods do not grant him any skill more than another. They never put their gifts into his hands, but they encompass and sustain him with their breath ... The true poem is not that which the public read. There is always a poem not printed on paper, coincident with the production of this, stereotyped in the poet's life. It is what he has become through his work. Now how is the idea expressed in stone, or on canvas or paper, is the question, but how far has it obtained form and expression in the life of the artist. His true work will not stand in any prince's gallery.

"My life has been the poem I would have writ,

---

[25] The full quotation is from <u>Ars Poetica</u>, and reads: "If you wish to draw tears from me, you must first feel pain yourself."
[26] From an essay of Carlyle's on Robert Burns.

> *But I could not both live and utter it.*
> *I hearing get, who had but ears,*
> *And sight, who had but eyes before,*
> *I moments live, who lived but years,*
> *And truth discern, who knew but learning's lore."* [27]

Notice that Carlyle inescapably links sincerity with enthusiasm and heartfelt emotion.

The two are truly inseparable. Thus Robert Graves writes:

> "Two hundred years ago a bishop approached the famous British actor David Garrick and inquired why clergymen "though believing what they preached, met with little response, while Garrick, knowing his subject to be only a fable, could rouse his audience."
>
> "Garrick replied that actors deliver their fictions with the warmth and energy of truth while ministers 'pronounce the most solemn truths with as much coldness and languor as if they were the most trivial fictions.'
>
> "Garrick was not suggesting that preachers be trained in theatrics, but that they deliver a living message with life ... Dwight Moody once wished his associate pastor could spend five minutes in hell. He knew such an experience would excite and motivate the most reserved preacher." [28]

But let enthusiasm be tempered by self-control, otherwise you might face the judgment given in 1887 by Richard Blackmore [29] on a preacher:

---

[27] "A Week on the Concord and Merrimac Rivers": The Heritage Press, CT, 1975 edition; pg. 279, 280, 285. The second poem is, I think, some lines from Ossian, a legendary Gaelic poet.
[28] From an article Preaching in the August 1986 "Advance" magazine.
[29] An English Novelist, most famous for Lorna Doone.

"(I found myself) sitting under the most furious distman that ever thumped a cushion."

So the general rule is this: preach only what you have personally experienced. We are not experts in everything. Some have sought to teach about "tongues" who have never spoken in tongues. Some want to become experts on divine healing, but they have never ministered healing by the power of the Spirit to anyone. Some "experts" on the family cannot seem to raise good kids.

Experience

> There are three ways to gain personal experience: immediately, vicariously, and scripturally.

Of course, you realize that you gain experience through things that happen in your own daily life. But you can also learn wisdom vicariously. You are not likely to live long enough to make all the mistakes yourself. In fact, you are allowed only one fatal one. You can learn from listening to teachers, through counseling others, and through friendship and fellowship. Scripturally, you gain "experience" through a real penetration of the message of scripture into your own spirit.

Avoid the mere parroting of other men's sermons. This was the common practice among carnal preachers in Judah, just before the Babylonian captivity. Jeremiah was preaching that judgment was coming, while everyone else in town was preaching peace and prosperity. Since they were the great majority, they were reassured in their error. Jeremiah was disgusted with the whole group, and so was God.

30 *"Therefore, behold, I am against the prophets, saith the LORD, that steal my words every one from his neighbour.*
31 *Behold, I am against the prophets, saith the LORD, that use their tongues, and say, He saith.*

> *32   Behold, I am against them that prophesy false dreams, saith the LORD, and do tell them, and cause my people to err by their lies, and by their lightness; yet I sent them not, nor commanded them: therefore they shall not profit this people at all, saith the LORD.*
> *33   And when this people, or the prophet, or a priest, shall ask thee, saying, What is the burden of the LORD? thou shalt then say unto them, What burden? I will even forsake you, saith the LORD.*
> *34   And as for the prophet, and the priest, and the people, that shall say, The burden of the LORD, I will even punish that man and his house.*
> *35   Thus shall ye say every one to his neighbour, and every one to his brother, What hath the LORD answered? and, What hath the LORD spoken?*
> *36   And the burden of the LORD shall ye mention no more: for every man's word shall be his burden; for ye have perverted the words of the living God, of the LORD of hosts our God.*
> *37   Thus shalt thou say to the prophet, What hath the LORD answered thee? and, What hath the LORD spoken?*
> *38   But since ye say, The burden of the LORD; therefore thus saith the LORD; Because ye say this word, The burden of the LORD, and I have sent unto you, saying, Ye shall not say, The burden of the LORD..."*[30]

The other prophets were artificially using Isaiah's phrase "the burden of the Lord". This is similar to preachers today who use the phrase "the Lord is saying to the church today..." because they heard someone else say it on a broadcast somewhere. The problem is that the other guy may have heard it second-hand from someone who made it up. This is not a problem that has only recently been resurrected. It has been going on for centuries.

Martin Luther saw the same problem during the Reformation of the sixteenth century.

---

[30] Jeremiah 23:30, 31, 33-38

> "Some pastors and preachers are lazy and no good. They rely on these and other good books to get a sermon out of them. They do not pray; they do not study; they do not read; they do not search the scripture. It is just as if there were no need to read the Bible for this purpose. They use such books as offer them homiletical helps in order to earn their yearly living; they are nothing but parrots and jackdaws, which learn to repeat without understanding ... Therefore the call is: watch, study, attend to reading. In truth you cannot read too much in scripture; and what you read you cannot read too carefully, and what you read carefully you cannot understand too well, and what you understand well you cannot teach too well ... He who has only one word of the Word of God and cannot preach a whole sermon on the basis of this one word is not worthy ever to preach!"[31]

Luther understood well the first key for overcoming "stage fright," or timidity in the pulpit. Some people have thought that they should come to the pulpit ignorant, so that God could fill their minds with divine thoughts. *"Open thy mouth, and I will fill it,"* was the excuse for many an uneducated and unstudied preacher whose sermons generated a lot more smoke than fire. God never encouraged ignorance or laziness. If you want to be a fluent speaker, know what you are talking about, and then practice your diction.

> "Who knows their subject can speak easily, for art follows comprehension of the subject. I can never compose a sermon by the rules of rhetoric." [32]

Martin Luther was not only a diligent student of the Word, he was also a man of prayer. The most important element of preaching is the anointing. Preaching is first and foremost speaking for God. In order to have a word for the people, you

---
[31] What Luther Says, volume 3, selections 3547, 3546.
[32] Table Talk of Martin Luther, ed. Thomas Kepler, Baker Book House, 1979

must pray. Prayer comes before study in the order of our priorities, and study of God's Word exceeds oratory skills in importance to the pulpiteer.

"When you are going to preach, first pray and say: 'Dear Lord, I would preach for thy honor; though I can do nothing good of myself, do thou make it good.' Don't think about Melancthon or Bugenhagen or me or any learned man, and don't try to be learned in the pulpit. I have never been troubled because I could not preach well, but I am overawed to think that I have to preach before God's face and speak of his infinite majesty and divine being. Therefore be strong and pray." [33]

"Let all your sermons be very plain and simple. Think not of the prince, but of the uncultivated and ignorant people. The prince himself is made of the same stuff as they! If in my preaching I should address myself to Philip I should do no good. I preach very simply to the uneducated and it suits everybody. Though I know Greek, Hebrew and Latin, these languages I keep for use among ourselves, and then we get them so twisted that our Lord God is amazed." [34]

---

[33] Ibid.
[34] Ibid.

Faith

You must approach your task with unshakable confidence in the power of the Word of God to bring life and fruit. Your faith must not be in your speaking ability, but in the living God Whose word you are declaring. Faith is not a function of the mind (positive thinking, sincere believing) as much as it is a function of the spirit. Faith involves a genuine focus on God and His purposes, as well as unshakable trust in His ability. Faith in "the faith message" can become a focus on positive thinking, and can become a form of presumption as we demand that God bend to our will, or as we "name it and claim it." Faith makes us the servant, not God.

As it relates to preaching, faith enables us to respond to the desires and direction of the Holy Spirit, rather than causing God to respond to our desires. You can preach with faith only when you know you have a word from God for the people you are addressing, rather than a "canned" speech that worked well when it was fresh. You are not out to make a good impression on the people. You are out to please the One who sent you with a message. Such faith can spring only out of an equally unshakable conviction that you are called to the task of preaching in this place at this time.

Anointing

The anointing has nothing to do with noise, sweat, rapid speech, emotion, tears, a superlative level of performance, or any other such observable phenomenon. Such things are commonly aroused in political orators, actors, athletes, gamblers, and others, who do not find it necessary to credit their surge of energy or skill to the Holy Spirit.

This does not mean that such phenomena are wrong or unnecessary, for they have their proper place in preaching as in other fields of human endeavor, but their source is natural adrenaline, not supernatural unction.

The popular concept of the anointing has little to do with the Biblical one. In Scripture, the anointing of God is primarily the "call of God"; that is, that act by which God sovereignly chooses a person for a particular task, and sets that person apart for that task.

I either have such an anointing or I do not. If I do have it, then the only thing required of me is to perform my God-given task to the best of my ability, with such obedience, prayer, faith, and toil as my particular calling in God may require. I am not going to waste time hunting around for some elusive, mysterious, indefinable, subjective afflatus. If I am diligently working to fulfill my God-given task, then I can be confident that my efforts will produce the extent of "harvest" he has ordained for me ("some thirty-fold, some sixty-fold, some a hundred-fold").

I am already "anointed." The thing to be determined at the *Bema* Throne (Judgment Seat of Christ) will be how well I have fulfilled the responsibility that came with that anointing. Anointing has more to do with appointing than it does with zeal. You may become a preacher because it was your saintly mother's dying wish, or because you have such a strong desire to be in full-time ministry. But, if God did not call you to preach, the ministry will always be a burden, and you will not produce lasting fruit. The call of God is always to a specific task. Actually, we generally think of the term "calling" in a different way than Jesus used it. He said,

> *"Ye have not chosen me, but I have chosen you, and ordained you, that ye should go and bring forth fruit, and that your fruit should remain: that whatsoever ye shall ask of the Father in my name, he may give it you."* [35]

Now, Jesus had said, *"Many are called, but few are chosen."* Some think that "chosen" refers to the fact that God chooses them to be saved. But Jesus used the word "chosen" in the sense that we generally use the word "called." Many were called to follow Jesus as His disciples, but only a few were chosen to be leaders (preachers). While we are all called of God to the ministry, we are not all chosen to be full-time preachers. Your call to preach is also

---
[35] John 15:16

not a reward for being spiritual and sincere. Some of the most sincere, dedicated people I know are factory workers, or janitors, or praying widows. But God has called some to be leaders and preachers, and they will all give an account to Him for the way they used that calling. You can use that mantle of the anointing to make yourself rich and famous; you can use it to control people to your advantage, but you will answer for it at the *Bema* throne. In eternity, it will be interesting to see who the "important" people will be.

If God anoints and appoints you to be a preacher, then you have a wonderful and awesome assignment in life. What you do with that anointing will determine your joy in life, and will affect your eternal reward. If you backslide, you will be a backslidden preacher.

A Willing Audience

People who want great preaching need to be great listeners. Preachers are influenced, even conditioned, by their audiences.

The story is told about a university class that decided to try an experiment: whenever the lecturer moved to the right of the platform, they gave all kinds of positive responses (nodding assent, sitting up, applause, etc.); but when he moved to the left, they gave a negative response (looking bored, yawning, stony-faced, slouching, and doodling on paper). After a few lectures, he was fixed to the right hand side of the platform, on the very edge.

Since the response of the people will have an affect on your ability to minister the Word, you need to do all you can to win their acceptance and gain their attention. Generally, it is more important for people to feel that you relate to them on a personal level than it is for them to regard you as an expert. They need to somehow feel that you care about them. Sharing personal experiences may seem like a waste of time, but they may help the people feel as if they know you personally, and that will help.

Sometimes, you have to earn the right to be heard. Ernest Weaver relates this experience.

"I was asked to teach a group of children on the role of the pastor. I thought, 'I've been involved in this for twenty-five years. I can teach on that any time.' I walked into the class after taking care of another job, and started talking to the group. I realized immediately that they were not with me. These rude kids were not paying attention to me! They were literally looking around the room, slouching, and even playing with each other's hair. They were used to being entertained, and I was not interesting. Unlike the adults in church, they did not feel obligated to make me think they were listening. I suddenly regretted the fact that I had not come prepared.

I then sang a witty song with a soundtrack, but they continued to sit, as if to say, "when is this guy going to shut up?" After fifteen miserable minutes, I moved to the piano and started to sing a song written by the Southern Baptist humorist, Dan McBride.

> 'Beautiful dreamer, wake unto me.
> I'm speaking to you there on pew number three.
> Sleeping in church is not for a deacon;
> 'Specially when I am up here and speakin'.
> Beautiful dreamer, don't start to snore.
> I've covered three points, but I've got four more.
> If you'll excuse me, I'll go ahead.
> But next Sunday why don't you stay home in bed.'

Instantly, the scene was changed. My bored, reluctant group of Sunday school prisoners perked up, and watched with fascination as I played skillfully on the keyboard. They strained to hear every word, and watched me with rapt attention. They had heard many adults come in and lecture them or sing with soundtracks, but no one had sung comedy songs with the piano before. I had their attention. I had earned the right to be heard. Now, I could tell them something about the subject, and they would listen to their friend."

Holy Ghost Power

Our aim is to be "Pentecostal" preachers (in the Biblical, not denominational, meaning of the term). Power is far more important that style. Our first aim is transformed lives by the power of the Spirit of God. We communicate truth that will set people free when we are charged by the unction of the Holy Spirit. When we are driven by a desire for a successful ministry, or for glory, we may have some personal "success," but we will have the spiritual fruitfulness of a true servant of God.

In Acts 17, we read the story of Paul the Apostle in Athens. There, he took on the intellectuals of his day, and proved to be a brilliant master of the art of debating. He presented a message that was clear and concise; a mental fortress of unimpeachable logic. He spoke to the intelligencia of the day in their own language. He beat them at their own game. But he had no converts that day.

Paul was not the last to make the mistake of pandering to the crowd. Eusebius (circa 730), for example, quotes a passionate letter written by the enemies of a bishop of Antioch during the latter part of the third century, Paul of Samosata. The bishop was apparently a marvelous orator who, despite humble origins, amassed vast wealth from his preaching. He loved pomp and splendor, encouraged the people to applaud his sermons, organized choirs of lovely young women to travel with him and to sing at his meetings, and furiously denounced other preachers. He was always surrounded by bodyguards, and sought the adulation of the crowds. If he were alive today, Eusebius would undoubtedly have his own syndicated television ministry and world outreach headquarters in southern Florida.

> *"But I will come to you shortly, if the Lord will, and will know, not the speech of them which are puffed up, but the power. For*

the kingdom of God is not in word, but in power." [36]

Power does not come from study or from practice. It also does not come from experience. Power comes from prayer. It comes to us as we spend hours in the presence of the Almighty, crying out to Him in humility and seeking His face. Power comes when He pours out the Holy Spirit, infusing our spirit with the "enablement" of the God of all grace.

This supernatural enablement for ministry is referred to as "grace" by the Apostle Paul. We have heard grace defined as "unmerited favor," but that is a weak, passive definition which does not do the term justice. Jesus was "full of grace and truth." He did not have "unmerited" favor. He had the power of the Holy Spirit flowing through His life, because He devoted Himself to prayer.

We are called to "grow in grace..". That is, we should become more and more dependent on the Spirit of God, and less dependent on our human skills and experience. Perhaps the best Biblical definition of grace is Philippians 2:13, which says, *"It is God that worketh in you, both to will and to do of His good pleasure."*

However, while style and skill are less important that the spiritual aspects of the ministry, they still affect the way in which people receive our message. If we are going to be effective communicators, we still need to learn principles of effective speaking.

Personal problems

Nerves

Some public speakers never overcome the distress of nervousness before they speak; others suffer it only in unfamiliar situations. We are generally suspicious of those who claim to be free of nervous tension. Their problem may rather be one of careless indifference.

---

[36] 1 Corinthians 4:20

Nervous tension can be your friend rather than your enemy. Consider the fact that the same power that immobilizes you can be changed into a source of energy. As the boy said to the neighborhood bully, "I can run faster scared than you can mad." Increased physical power can come out of a state of tension. If you are not nervous, you will still have to stir up the energy level that nerves would have produced.

Two Kinds of Nervous Tension

Positive nervous tension.

God created His creatures with a "flight or fight" mechanism. When danger threatens, an animal will experience a surge of adrenaline. This immediately shuts down the flow of blood to the gastrointestinal system, and increases the blood flow to the voluntary muscles, heart, and brain. We feel some stress, our heart beats faster, our mind is clearer. Our senses are more alert. The positive tension makes us alert and strong. It can also motivate us to pray.

Negative nervous tension.

This kind of tension comes generally from the fear of failure. *"The fear of man brings a snare."* [37] The fear of failure can be immobilizing. The body does not know the difference between a

---

[37] Proverbs 29:25

perceived physical threat (mortal danger) and an emotional threat (the people in the audience do not like me). Some people whose lives are dominated by fear will avoid any endeavor if it involves risk. Since nothing is accomplished without risk, the fear results in the very thing feared, because, if you do not do anything, you are guaranteed to fail in life. It is vital that we learn to fear God more than we fear people, failure, injury, or death.

What would you suggest as ways to cure this negative nervousness? Martin Luther, while he was still a novice in the Catholic monastery, was once given some drastic counsel on the problem by his monastic superior, Dr. Staupitz.

> "Ah, my friend," Luther later said to another young and nervous preacher, "... I feared the pulpit perhaps as greatly as you do; yet I had to do it. I was forced to preach ... Ah! how I feared the pulpit! ... Under this very pear tree I advanced more than fifteen arguments to Dr. Staupitz (as to why I should not preach). With (those arguments) I declined my call. But they did me no good. When I finally said, 'Dr. Staupitz, you are taking my life; I shall not live a quarter-year,' he replied: 'In God's name! Our Lord God has many things to do; he is in need of wise people in heaven too!'" [38]

The basic problem with nervous preachers is that we are more self-conscious than God-conscious. We are so concerned with how we are being received and perceived that we lose sight of the message. The important thing is that people receive the Gospel! The ideal state of mind for preaching is to be so focused on God and His purposes, and so full of the Word, that we forget about ourselves. We need to realize that we are messengers, and Jesus is the message. We are vessel, and He is the all-important treasure.

When Jesus began to gain in popularity among the people, some of John's disciples were concerned for the success of his

---

[38] <u>What Luther Says</u>, volume 3, pg. 1110

ministry. Some people were leaving John to follow Jesus. John replied,

"He must increase, but I must decrease." [39]

---

[39] John 3:30

Either he's really anointed, or
he's been eating at Casa Maria's again.

PRACTICUM

Voice interlude

It is possible to improve your voice in four areas: pitch, dynamics, volume, and penetration.

Pitch Relax your voice to as low and melodious a level as you can reach without strain. Since nervousness tends to tighten the muscles, the voice will be affected by a higher pitch. A low voice is, therefore, soothing, and more pleasant to the listener.

Dynamics (compass): ranging from high tones to low.
Some people think of a "dynamic" speaker as one who is loud and boisterous. But a genuinely dynamic speaker will have a wide range of expressions, so that he can articulate the words in moods appropriate to the thoughts. If he is loud all the time, he will be monotonous and irritating. If he uses a good range of vocal pitch, volume, and style, he will be more likely to hold the attention of the listeners, as well as emphasize the important points.

Volume is controlled softness and loudness.
You need to be heard without being overbearing or irritating.

Penetration (projection): not the same as volume.
A good speaker will be able to project his voice for a distance without straining his voice. This is done by using the diaphragm, the muscle which supports the lungs. If you preach a loud sermon without good vocal technique, your throat will be sore. You should be able to speak or sing for hours without hurting your voice. Your stomach muscles and diaphragm may be sore, but your throat will be fine. Most of the force should come from the diaphragm, which you naturally use when coughing, laughing, yawning, and breathing while lying on your back. Try the syllable: Chow!

Resonate your voice from the hard palate at the top of your mouth, instead of from the fleshy back parts of the throat. Some sounds come naturally from the hard palate and resonate in the upper bony structure, such as "Oo!" and "let." Contrast those sounds with "Ah." Then, without changing the position of the sounds, say in succession, "Oo! Ah! Oo! Ah!" To develop resonance, begin by humming, then pronounce the syllable "Maw!"

Develop variety by the following formula:

- higher - lower
- softer - louder
- faster - slower

Some appropriate quotations:

A preacher should have the following qualifications:

1. The ability to teach.
2. A good mind.
3. Eloquence.
4. A good voice.
5. A good memory.
6. The power to leave off (a.k.a. the sense to quit when finished).
7. Diligence.
8. Whole-souled devotion to his calling.
9. Willingness to take time for people's individual needs.
10. Patience to bear all things.

"In ministers nothing is seen more easily or more quickly than their faults. A preacher may have a hundred virtues, yet they may all be obscured by a single defect, the world is now so bad. Dr. Jonas has all the attributes of a good preacher, but people cannot forgive the good man for hawking and spitting so often." [40]

---

[40] Luther, quoted by Kapler, op. cit.

Can you think of some irritating habits you have observed in preachers?

On Long Sermons

> "It is commonly said these are the three qualifications that mark a good preacher: first, that he step up; second, that he speak up, and say something worthwhile; third, that he know when to stop ... To preach long is no art; but to preach and to teach right well, that is work, that is labor!" [41]

> Put another way: **get up, speak up, and shut up.**

> "To me a long sermon is an abomination, for the desire of the audience to listen is destroyed, and the preacher only defeats himself. On this account I took Dr. Bugenhagen severely to task, for although he preaches long sermons with spontaneity and pleasure, nevertheless it is a mistake." [42]

There is indeed no special virtue in length. Luther's sermons (not his lectures) rarely exceeded 30 minutes (cp. Robert Schuller). Even Spurgeon kept to within one hour. More humble preachers would be wiser to say two or three worthwhile things in less than thirty minutes than to punish the people with a sixty-minute mash of repetitions.

If you are under a cultural obligation to speak for forty minutes or more, make sure you put in the requisite study (One great preacher reckoned he needed an hour of study for every minute of sermon!). Remember also: you are more likely to receive divine guidance at home in your study than you are at the pulpit.

---

[41] <u>What Luther Says</u>, Volume 3, pg. 1110
[42] Kepler, op. cit.

On Rambling Sermons

On a famous preacher's tendency to wander from his text, Luther remarked:

> "Bugenhagen says whatever occurs to him. Jonas used to say, 'Don't hail every soldier you meet.' That is right. Bugenhagen often takes along everyone whom he meets with him. Let him take care to keep to the text and attend to what is before him and make people understand that. Those preachers who say whatever comes into their mouths remind me of a maid going to market. When she meets another maid she stops and chats a while, then she meets another and talks with her, too, and then a third and a fourth, and so gets to market very slowly. So with preachers who wander off the text; they would like to say everything at one time, but they can't ...
> "When Morlin, Medler, or Jacob preaches, it is just as when the plug is drawn from a full cask; the liquid runs out as long as there is any left within. But such volubility of tongue doesn't really lay hold of the audience, though it delights some, nor is it even instructive. It is better to speak distinctly, so that what is said may be comprehended." [43]

Disappointment

Here are some passages from St. Augustine. ((He is instructing a gifted speaker who nonetheless had become frustrated by apparent failure.)

> "You have made confession and complaint that it has often befallen you that in the course of a lengthened and languid address you have become profitless and distasteful even to yourself, not to speak of the learner whom you have been endeavoring to instruct by your utterance, and the other parties who have been present as hearers ...

---

[43] ibid.

> One thing which I have heard you make the subject of your complaint above all others, is the fact that your discourse seemed to yourself to be poor and spiritless when you were instructing any one in the Christian name ... "Indeed, with me, too, it is almost always the fact that my speech displeases myself. For I am covetous of something better, the possession of which I frequently enjoy within me before I commence to body it forth in intelligible words; and then when my capacities of expression prove inferior to my inner apprehensions, I grieve over the inability which my tongue has betrayed in answering to my heart. For it is my wish that he who hears me should have the same complete understanding of the subject which I have myself; and I perceive that I fail to speak in a manner calculated to effect that ... " [44]

On another cause of frustration, Augustine writes:

> "A sense of weariness is also induced upon the speaker when he has a hearer who remains unmoved, either in that he is actually not stirred by any feeling, or in that he does not indicate by any motion of the body that he understands or that he is pleased with what is said. Not that it is a becoming disposition in us to be greedy of the praises of men, but that the things which we minister are of God; and the more we love those to whom we discourse, the more desirous we are that they should be pleased with the matters which are held forth for their salvation: so that if we do not succeed in this, we are pained, and we are weakened, and become broken-spirited in the midst of our course, as if we were wasting our efforts to no purpose." [45]

So resolve now neither to be deterred nor discouraged by failure, whether real or imagined!

---

[44] Post-Nicene Fathers, volume 3, pg. 283, 292, 284.
[45] Ibid. pg. 293

Chapter Four

The Direction for a Sermon

Effective communication

There are five parts to good communication.
Good communication is moral, ethical, emotional, rational, and practical.

The Moral

The content of the message should reflect the good character of the speaker, without guile, genuine and sincere. This is always the most convincing part of the argument. Ultimately, we want to promote the moral standards of the Bible, regardless of the mores of the generation in which we live. God's Word does not change with the culture.

> *"The lips of the righteous feed many: but fools die for want of wisdom."* [46]

> *"Wherewithall shall a young man cleanse his way? by taking heed thereto according to thy word."* [47]

The Ethical

The speaker should be competent, accurate, and qualified. He should treat others with respect, and communicate directly and quickly with those who are in conflict with him. He should honor the authority of the church he is in, and respect the people to whom he ministers. The man of God should always see himself as a servant, and not the master over the people.

> *"And the servant of the Lord must not strive; but be gentle unto all men, apt to teach, patient, in meekness instructing those that oppose themselves..."* [48]

---

[46] Proverbs 10:21
[47] Psalm 119:9
[48] II Timothy 2:24-25a

> "Neither as being lords over God's heritage, but being ensamples to the flock." [49]

The Emotional

A good preacher is constantly reaching the hearts of the hearers, striving for a response. As one old southern preacher put it, "I know you can't go on feelings, but praise God you can feel what you're goin' on."

We are emotional creatures. Our emotions affect every aspect of our life and personality. There is a time to move people to tears, and a time to move them to laughter. The Apostle Paul moved the people in Corinth to sorrow. It was good, because it motivated them to repent. The Apostle Jude said,

> "...and of some have compassion, making a difference:
> And others save with fear, pulling them out of the fire..." [50]

The Rational

When we preach the Word, we are appealing to the mind as well as the spirit, reaching for conviction of the truth. Contrary to what some believe, the Gospel is not irrational. We do not reject logic when we embrace faith; we transcend it, and respond to the Truth that is rooted in the spiritual and reflected in the physical world. Viewed from the standpoint of the secular humanist, the Word is "foolishness," because he cannot see spiritual things with the natural mind, [51] and he is spiritually blind.

> "Except a man be born again, he cannot see (the kingdom of heaven)." [52]

> "For we have not followed cunningly devised fables, when we made known unto

---

[49] I Peter 5:3
[50] Jude 22-23
[51] I Corinthians 2:14
[52] John 3:3

> you the power and coming of our Lord Jesus Christ, but were eyewitnesses of his majesty." [53]

The Practical

The effective preacher must consistently make the message relevant to the hearers. The Gospel is real truth that applies to a real world. People need answers, and the Bible has them. Christians need "instruction in righteousness." They need teaching about relationships, money, morality, and life in general. Jesus was spiritual, but He also met the real needs of people. People are not interested in your high-sounding theories about the eschatological implications of the Persian Gulf War. They need to know how to overcome discouragement, sin, and guilt.

> *"All scripture is given by inspiration of God, and is profitable for doctrine, for reproof, for correction, for instruction in righteousness; that the man of God may be perfect, thoroughly furnished unto all good works."* [54]

Note: One of the worst sins you can commit is to bore your audience! God forbid that your hearers would ever react as his companions did to the Monk, who had spun a gloomy tale, or rather, preached a dreary sermon to them.

"'Ho, my good sir, no more!" exclaimed the Knight;
'What you have said so far no doubt is right,
And more than right, but still, a little grief
Will do for most of us, in my belief ... '
"Our Host joined in. 'This Monk, he talks too loud;
All about "Fortune covered with a cloud" ...
Let's have no more of it. God bless you, master,
It's an offense, you're boring us, that's why!
Such talk as that's not worth a butterfly,
Gives no enjoyment, doesn't help the game,
In short Sir Monk - Sir Peter - what's-your-name,
I heartily beg you'll talk of something else.

---

[53] II Peter 1:16
[54] II Timothy 3:16-17

But for the clink and tinkle of those bells
That hand your bridle round on every side,
By my salvation, by the Lord that died,
I simply should have fallen down asleep
Into the mud below, however deep.
Your story then would have been told in vain,
For, quoting the authorities again,
"When lecturers find their audiences decrease,
It does them little good to say their piece."
Give us a word or two on hunting, say.'
"No," said the Monk, "I'm in no mood today
For fun. Ask someone else. I've said enough."' [55]

I don't think you fellows are giving my ministry the respect it deserves. Now come on. Get with it!

The Whole Counsel of God

"And how I kept back nothing that was profitable unto you, but have showed you, and have taught you publicly, and from house to house," [56]

---

[55] The Canterbury Tales, by Geoffrey Chaucer; translated by Nevill Coghill; Penguin Classics, 1977
[56] Acts 20:20

The "Hobby Horse" Syndrome.

One of the functions of a pastor is to feed the "sheep" a balanced diet. Teachers are generally "specialists" who come in for a few meetings and focus on an area of study upon which they have made an intensive search. But the pastor needs to be careful that he does not spend too much of his time on a certain area. For example, a pastor may be a giver, and will love to preach on missions giving and tithing. But if the people are discouraged, or if their marriages are falling apart, they may leave the church, looking for someone to meet that need in their family.

Some pastors plan the sermon themes a year in advance, seeking to cover as many areas of Biblical study as possible. They seek the Lord to find the needs of the people, and then prepare the "menu" for the year. Sadly, there are some who look at the needs of the "organization," and meditate on ways to get the people to meet the needs of the "church." But most pastors are genuinely concerned about the needs of the people, and seek to meet them.

It is also a good policy to realize that no preacher has all the insights on every topic. We should all be aware of our weak areas, and bring in outside speakers who are strong where we are not. If, for instance, you are a very evangelistic pastor, then you should bring in some outstanding teachers, or raise up a few teachers in the congregation. If you are strong in teaching, then be sure to bring in prophets or evangelists. The goal is for each local church to be influenced by the "five-fold" ministry on a regular basis. This will help to insure balance. There are some unfortunate churches with a leader who is so insecure that he cannot bring in any outside ministry for fear that he might not hold on to his position. He will probably lose it sooner or later, because the people won't stay long.

The "hobby horse" is, of course, the excessive focus on one theme or issue. Preachers who make this common mistake are, for whatever reason, insensitive to the needs of the people. Often, they continually refer to a topic because it is an area of ongoing failure in their personal life, and they are plagued with personal guilt. The key is to concentrate on meeting the needs of the families you serve, rather than on yourself.

The "Final Answer" Syndrome

Preachers should be prepared and confident relating to their subject matter, but there is always the danger of becoming so dogmatic and egoistic that the people feel alienated and disregarded. It is important for us to put our confidence in the Lord, and remind ourselves that the Bible is the final authority on truth, and not our own minds. We should never try to convince people that we know all the answers. In fact, it is a good idea to say "I don't know" occasionally when you come to an area for which you have little or no revelation, or upon which we have done little study. Some preachers have been extremely embarrassed because they tried to give people the impression that they were Greek scholars, or expert on some subject, and then were exposed in some fashion.

Give the Lord Your Best

By all means, use every art and skill that is available to you, and all the tools and resources at your command. Remember that God gives us opportunities to learn and study, but we have to be diligent to develop and use the gifts (or talents, if you prefer) in order to teach and train others. Always keep a servant's heart. Use your music or speaking skills to minister to others, but be careful not to use your abilities with a motive to exalt yourself.

Many people live life by saying, "If only I had his advantages. If only I could have been...." Joseph is one of many Bible heroes who could have been bitter. He was destined for greatness. He had a divine mandate, but his own brothers, moved with envy, sold him into slavery. His response: "I did not choose this, and I don't understand it, but God is God. If I am going to be a slave, then I'll be the best slave in Egypt." And he was. His "reward" was a false accusation and a prison sentence. His response: "If I'm going to be a prisoner, then I'll be the best prisoner in Egypt." He gave his best, and God honored him for it.

Some Christians seem to put more zeal and energy into their sports than into their ministry. We need to realize that Jesus is rightly the central focus of life, and that we should be more excited about eternal things than about any temporal activity or reward.

The best music belongs to God. The best we have is the only appropriate gift to give back to Him who gave us His all.

Chapter Five

Preparing a Message

Step One: Think and Pray about the Theme.

- ☐ What does the Holy Spirit want?
- ☐ What do the people need? Where do they need correcting, instructing, encouraging, or assisting?
- ☐ The "theme" may be a topic or a text, or a combination of both -- (that is, a topic built around a text).

A common, though usually unexpressed, diversion is to think, "what am I really good at preaching? What will get the best response? What will move the people to give the most money? What will sell the most books or tapes? This sounds cynical, but it happens all the time. We need to guard our hearts against the self-serving temptations of the flesh, and keep our eyes on the goal. Do we want the people to think of me as a great preacher, or are we more concerned with elevating their opinion of Jesus?

Also, we need to keep our priorities in order. First, determine the will and direction of the Holy Spirit, then think about the needs of the people. You are probably aware of specific needs, but there will always be some of which you are not fully aware. The Spirit is always aware of the needs of the people.

When you have a theme, you will have a direction and purpose at which to aim. You will usually have an idea of the response you will seek to encourage throughout the message. You must always have a purpose beyond "preach next Sunday."

Step Two: Develop that Theme.

- ☐ Research the topic or text, accumulating several pages of notes.
- ☐ Look up definitions of key words in the Greek and English dictionaries.
- ☐ Check out cross-referenced Bible passages, and read about related topics.

- ☐ Think earnestly and creatively about ways to arrange the material in order to develop an effective sermon outline.

Example: Pride.

- ☐ What are the Greek and Hebrew words for "pride" used in the Old and New Testaments?
- ☐ What are their definitions?
- ☐ How are the different words used in the Bible?
- ☐ In what context are they used?
- ☐ What Bible characters illustrate the principle that "pride goeth before destruction."? (King Saul, Herod, etc.)
- ☐ What are outstanding examples of the strength of humility?
- ☐ In fact, what does "humility" really mean?
- ☐ Is it the most direct counterpart to pride?
- ☐ What are some other historical characters that demonstrated some truths about the danger of pride? (Nero, Napoleon, Adolf Hitler, Bill Clinton, etc.)

Make an Outline.

An outline is the "skeleton" of any good message. It defines the principle ideas which support and amplify the theme, and establishes the structure. There are several key benefits to beginning with an outline.

- ☐ An outline is an aid to the speaker's memory.

- ☐ An outline helps the people to follow the message better.

- ☐ It helps to prevent the speaker from rambling (getting sidetracked on relative ideas that will detract from the ultimate goal of the message)

- ☐ An outline helps the speaker control his time better. (You can assess the length of a message from its outline.)

- What turns a pile of building materials into a house?
- What turns a heap of organic ingredients into a meal?
- What transforms a collection of sounds into music?

Arrangement!

A good arrangement (or outline) requires concentrated, creative thinking. Some speakers are plainly more gifted at this than others, and each person is more gifted at some times than at others. But hard work will improve anyone.

A good outline will have:

Color: This relates to interest, drama, impact, and curiosity value.

Unity: Each part belongs to the theme, and supports it. There is nothing extraneous or irrelevant in the outline. A good outline is more than just three or four sermonettes strung together, or a group of passages with the same word in them.

Sequence: Each section should flow naturally into the next. Give attention to the "links" in your outline.

Balance: No one part should have a disproportionate amount of space. Do not over-emphasize unimportant points.

Conclusion. The beginning and end should both be planned. The end is more important than the beginning. Make it a true climax, not a feeble anti-climax.

Stories: Meat on the Skeleton.

Good speakers collect ideas, anecdotes, quotations, themes, etc., and keep them on file for later use. A preacher who relies on his memory will usually see it fail when he is in need of a good story to color a drab sermon. Written notes are wonderfully helpful, but only if they are filed in such as way that you can find them.

A reading program in fiction, history, poetry, drama, and theology is essential for this purpose. You must be a continual student of the Bible, but there are rich resources for further illustration in history. All of true history reinforces the basic principles of Scripture. God's Word is true, and His principles never fail. We can learn many lessons from the failures of wicked people, especially if they are not obscured by revisionist historians.

Anecdotes from your own experience can be very effective in establishing a personal link with the audience. However, if there are too many, you may come across as egocentric. A good balance is to relate personally to the theme without an excessive emphasis on self.

****

PRACTICUM

Prepare a three-minute "talk to get action".
Your talk must have three parts:

- ❏ Share a moving or dramatic incident from your own life (2 minutes).

- ❏ Lead into something you want the people to do relating to that incident (30 seconds).

- ❏ Show them the benefit they can expect if they respond positively to your exhortation (30 seconds).

Example:
>"I once enjoyed a powerful day of prayer and fasting ...
>You too should have such a day...
>These are the benefits you will gain... " (Read from Isaiah 58.)

****

Choosing a Scripture Text

The word text is from the Latin "Textus" or "taxtum", signifying something woven or spun...

The text is not a mere motto, and should not be chosen after the theme or subject and the finished sermon. The sermon should be woven from the text. It also should go without saying that every sermon should be based on a Bible text. It does not necessarily have to be the King James Version, but it should be the Bible. If it sounds strange to mention this, then you should know that some preachers, seeking to be "relevant," have used magazine articles, secular books, or their own writings as a "text." If you have a message but cannot find a Bible text to support it, then throw that message in file thirteen (the round one on the floor).

"The length of the text depends upon the circumstances and usage." Sometimes a lengthy text is necessary, and will almost preach itself. Of course, the length of the reading text is also greatly influenced by the allotted time for the sermon.

Advantages of Finding the Right Text for the Message:

- ☐ The right text awakens the interest of the audience.
- ☐ It gains the confidence of the audience (God's opinion and not yours).
- ☐ It gives the preacher authority and boldness. "Thus saith the Lord."
- ☐ It keeps the preacher's mind from wandering.
- ☐ It helps to keep the preacher from straying into error.

Choosing a text depends on two things: the preacher's own mind, and the idea of the sermon. If the preacher's mind is barren and sterile, dry and empty, choosing the text will be hard. If on the other hand, his mind and soul are steeped in truth, daily fellowship with God, choosing a text will be easy. Sermons should be straight from the heart of the preacher to the soul of the hearers.

The sermon will begin either with a topical idea, or with a text. Ideally, a preacher will often find in his personal devotional time that a passage from the Bible will be "quickened" in his spirit. That is, the Holy Spirit will make it suddenly alive and powerful, and he will have a rush of ideas as to how that thought can motivate people to pursue after the things of God.

Be careful, by the way, to maintain times of personal devotion. Read the Bible daily, and not just when you need to get a sermon for the next service. It is possible to be a preacher and personally dry up spiritually. Draw from the "wells of salvation" daily for your own edification.

If your sermon begins with a topic, be sure to look for a Bible text that directly relates to the idea you need to present. Don't just thumb through a concordance and pull out verses with a common word. Find the text that communicates best what you need to share, and then find the cross-reference texts that will support it. Also, be familiar with the surrounding material related to the selected text. The rest of the writing is called the "context." As someone wisely noted,

"A text without a context is a pretext."

General Principles about Preaching

Carefully consider the spiritual needs of the people to whom you minister. Study your people. Think about their physical, mental, moral, spiritual needs. Of course, this is secondary to the consideration of "what is the Holy Spirit wanting to say?" Or, put another way, "What would Jesus say if He were here?" He is, and He can speak through you. Your work is to be His messenger. The people are not really there to hear your ideas. If they come to church, they want to see Jesus, and nothing less will do. Having said that, we realize that our second consideration is the needs of the people. The last thing you want to consider is your own needs. (Will this go over big and get me a good love offering? Will I be admired and rewarded? Is this a funny sermon that the people will like?)

What should I preach about?

Make a careful consideration of the cycle of truth preached. What themes have I developed lately? Am I including doctrine? Are all my sermons on salvation? Do I get on a tangent upon a certain line and stay there?

There are some outstanding preachers who will take a few days of fasting and prayer to plan the "menu" for the next year's preaching. They will look for balance, and try to cover the basics, determined by the spiritual needs of the people. Considering the fact that most of people listening will be Christians, it is unfair to them to direct too much of the sermon to the unsaved. Perhaps it is better to feed the "sheep" so that they can be equipped to bear the lambs.

Some preachers have the mentality that they need to get people in so that they can build the church. This is a wrong focus. The people are not there to serve the preacher. The preacher is there to build up the families, and to equip the saints for the work of the ministry. If you build the families by disciplining men and setting the example of a good marriage and home, the strong families will result in a strong church. When you build the people up and help them become successful in life, they will make you successful.

Here is a valuable question to consider: what does the Bible emphasize? For instance, we have thousands of songs about the "mansion" mentioned in John 14. There is very little in scripture concerning the house that Jesus is building for us, but there are volumes concerning the place we are to build for God's habitation (the tabernacle and temple as types of the church: Ephesians 2:20)

Some general topics that should get attention on a regular basis

- Salvation, Sin, and Righteousness.
- Sanctification and holiness (instruction in righteousness)
- Marriage and relationships (provoke one another to love and to good works)
- Eschatology (Jesus is coming again)
- Judgment and accountability
- The person and work of the Holy Spirit
- The value and purpose of water baptism and communion.
- The baptism in the Holy Spirit.
- Personal evangelism.
- The successful home and family.
- Knowing God's will.
- A servant's heart.
- The tongue.
- Tithing, giving, and good money management.
- Conquering bitterness, fear, and discouragement.
- Joy in the Holy Ghost
- Seek ye first the Kingdom of God...
- Overcoming temptation.

Particular Principles

Read the Bible

Read it daily with diligence and delight. Study it as your most important textbook for life. It is not merely a textbook; it is a book of texts. You may not feel that you are "getting something out if it" every time you pick it up, but the Bible ministers beyond your mind. It speaks to your spirit. That's the uniqueness of the Bible. It is not written to the carnal mind. Jesus said,

> *"It is the spirit that quickeneth; the flesh profiteth nothing: the words that I speak unto you, they are spirit, and they are life."* [57]

Use a Notebook

Read with a notebook in your hand. Whenever an illustration, thought or argument impresses you, make a note of it. Jot down important thoughts as they come to you.

Read inspirational books

Books about the Bible are no substitute for the real thing, but they can be an excellent supplement to your Bible reading, especially if they include accurate historical accounts. Never read to copy them, but to inspire your own mind. Read the lives of great preachers, missionaries, and reformers. Research historical references.

Seek the guidance of the Holy Spirit.

You will never be at a loss for something to preach if you are in tune with the Spirit. The Holy Spirit always has something to say. It is only our hearing that is intermittent.

---

[57] John 6:63

Precautions in the Choice of Texts

Do not focus on trying to be clever with your titles and texts.

Examples:

- ☐ A sermon to a group of tailors, the minister took for his text: "A remnant shall be saved."
- ☐ To a group of news reporters, "And he sought to see Jesus who he was and could not for the press."
- ☐ To a group of judges, "Judge not, and ye shall not be judged."
- ☐ Against women coiling their hair on top of their heads, the text was, "Top-knot come down!" from Matt. 24. "Let him which is on the house-top not come down."
- ☐ A sermon on Naaman called "Seven ducks in a muddy river."

Try not to be obvious or trite.

If you're preaching in a prison, do not automatically go to Paul and Silas in Jail," or "The Truth Shall Set You Free." Somebody just may have shared that with them before.

Do not choose a text which in view of surrounding circumstances will make it appear ridiculous.

A minister, newly-married, after the visit to his bride's home convulsed his congregation with laughter by announcing for his text, "Oh that I were in months past."

A preacher of great physical proportions and huge sheaf of notes placed upon two Bibles, rose to full height and said: "Thou shalt see greater things than these."

Do not choose questionable texts

An example would be John 9:31 "We know that God heareth not sinners." This was spoken by the blind man, not by the Holy Spirit. God does hear sinners (remember the Publican in temple?) when they pray a prayer of repentance.

Do not use mutilated texts.

Avoid using only parts of verses e.g. "All men are liars," or, "There is no God." Satan's first lie was half-truth. He said if Adam and Eve would eat of the fruit, their eyes would be opened. They were, but it was to see themselves as sinners. The Bible records history accurately, including some things spoken by the devil or evil men. Consider that not everything spoken by Job's friends was true, but it is all truly recorded. Everything quoted from God in the Bible is true, but every statement by the devil is a lie.

Do not neglect the Old Testament.

The Old Testament is also the inspired Word of God.

"All Scripture is...profitable for...doctrine". [58]

When Paul used the term "scripture," he was referring to the Old Testament. The New Testament didn't exist yet. If you throw out the Old Testament, you are discarding most of God's Word. Remember, Jesus did not discount the Old Testament. He said,

"Think not that I am come to destroy the law, or the prophets: I am not come to destroy, but to fulfil." [59]

---

[58] II Timothy 3:16
[59] Matthew 5:17

Interpretation of the Text

Rules for the Interpretation of a Text.

Ascertain whether the language of the text is literal or figurative.

The Bible is full of analogies, symbols, and types, particularly in prophetic books. It is not written to the mind, but to the spirit. The devil cannot figure out the Revelation. We cannot either, but we are blessed by reading it. We do not always know when things are symbolic or literal, but we do get a sense of who Jesus is, and who wins in the end.

Figurative

> Jesus said to the Jews -- *"Destroy this Temple, and in three days I will raise it up."* John 2:19 - 22.
> Also, in the Lord's Supper, the bread and wine were not flesh and blood, but were symbols. The Bible does not teach transubstantiation.
> (See Matthew 26:26 -27, Mark 14:22-24, Luke 22:19 -20,
> and I Corinthians 11:23-26.)
> Jesus is pictured in Revelation 1 with white hair, brass feet, and eyes of fire. White is a symbol of holiness, brass symbolizes judgment, etc.

Literal

> Luke 16, Jesus told of a real man named Lazarus, who went to a real place called Paradise. He also told of the rich man who went to a real hell. It was not an allegory.
> Adam and Eve were real people, who lived in a real garden, and ate a real banana...

Ascertain the meanings of words used by each writer of the Scriptures.

All writers do not give the same word exactly the same meaning. The word "faith" in Galatians 1:23, I Timothy 3:9, and Acts 24:24 means the Gospel in which faith in Christ is the great doctrine. It is not a generic word meaning trust or confidence. In Romans 3:3, the word "faith" means truth, or the faithfulness of God in keeping His Word. In Acts 17:31 it means proof or evidence. In Romans 14:23 it means conscientious conviction of duty.

The word "flesh" in Ezekiel 11:19 is used in contrast to stone, and is a positive reference. In John 1:14 and Romans 1:3, 9:3, "flesh" refers to the carnal human nature, as opposed to "spirit". In that context, "flesh" is a negative term.

The word "salvation" in Exodus 14:13 means outward safety or deliverance. In James 5:15, it is referring to bodily healing. Actually, the Greek word for "salvation" means "to make whole," and can refer to wholeness of spirit, soul, or body. It does not refer to a ticket to heaven. It relates to the forgiveness and transformation of mind that accompanies the new birth, and eventually results in heaven, but is not synonymous with eternal life. In Romans 13:11, "salvation" speaks of the whole blessing which Christ has for believers. In Hebrews 2:3, it means the simple gospel of Jesus Christ.

Note also that there are often different words translated into English to the same word, and each will have a distinctive meaning. Or, a Greek word may be translated with several different English words. Always look first to the concordance and Greek (or Hebrew) dictionary to accurately define a word. As a secondary resource, look it up in an English dictionary.

Understanding a word from the context.

The word "perfection" in Psalm 37:37 means "uprightness, sincerity," "unfeigned goodness" as opposed to "sham goodness". In the New Testament it means "possession of the clear truth". In James 1:4 the word "perfection" means "entire, lacking nothing".

Sometimes words are to be understood according to context to mean the very opposite of their usual sense. In I Kings 22:15 *"Go and prosper"* is spoken ironically, and the prophet meant the reverse. Micaiah knew that King Ahab would die in the battle, but he also knew what he wanted to hear. In Numbers 22:20 it means

"Rise up and go". In verse 12 and 32; it means "do it at your own risk".

Circumstances

In what circumstances was the writer? We can gain tremendous insight by understanding the culture, politics, and geography surrounding the writings and the writers of scripture. We cannot appreciate the intense strain between the Jews and Romans unless we understand the fact that the Jews were literally slaves of Rome, with very little freedom. We cannot get the full impact of the "Good Samaritan" unless we realize the ongoing animosity between Jews and Samaritans, and the general reputation of the despised latter group.

We should also be aware of the character of the people at the time of writing. King David was surrounded by some fascinating people. The more we know about them, the more accurately we can apply the truths illustrated by their lives and their relationships. Also, note the co-workers and enemies mentioned in the writings of Paul. Most of them are relatively obscure, but they are all interesting.

Prooftext

We compare scripture with scripture in order to arrive at its true meaning. Cults arrive at wrong doctrines generally by taking individual phrases or verses and draw conclusions from them. These are generally led by individuals who, answering to no one, look at the Bible from their own frame of reference, and find verses to support their own notions about God. They are not guided by the Teacher (Holy Spirit), and are often encouraged by the kingdom of darkness.

In order to "rightly divide the word of truth," we need to be familiar with the Bible as a whole, and understand the basic tenor of truth, which makes it consistent with itself. No verse stands alone. Every truth in God's Word is reinforced by more than one mention. Cross-references are important, but note that they are not infallible. That is, a writer may think that two verses are related, only because he misunderstood one of them. The more we know the whole Bible, the better equipped we are to "compare spiritual things with spiritual." [60]

Example:

Proverbs 16:4: *"The Lord hath made all things for himself; yea, even the wicked for the day of evil".* (The doctrine that the wicked were created that they might be condemned is inconsistent with innumerable parts of the Scripture, and therefore cannot be true. God created everything, and allowed angels and men freedom of choice, but He did not dictate that choice. *"God is not willing that any should perish.")*

See Psalm 145:9, Ezekiel 18:23 and II Peter 3:9, meaning that all evil shall contribute to the glory of God and promote the accomplishment of His magnificent design.

A Knowledge of the Manners and Customs of the People to Whom the Bible was Originally Written.

What kind of homes did people live in back in those days? Some lived in caves, and some had "poor mud huts befitting images of the frailty of human life". (Job 24:6 and Matthew 6:19) There was no electricity.

Rich people may have had houses with flat roof porches, porticos, and guest chambers. How do we picture Peter on a roof praying and sleeping? It could not have been like my roof! He would have rolled off. Pitched roofs were not common in those days. That explains the need for guardrails in the early days of Israel. [61]

Consider their dress. People generally wore two garments: one was a close-bodied frock extending a little below the knees. Then they had an outer garment that was a long, loose robe. Inside, they were wrapped in a simple under-garment. To wear only this was regarded as a state of undress; hence persons clothed in it alone are said to be naked. Isaiah 20:2-4 and John 13:4. By understanding

---

[60] I Corinthians 2:13
[61] See Mark 13:15, Acts 10:9 and Deuteronomy 22:8.

this, we do not have to visualize Isaiah or Jesus appearing publicly naked as many have inferred from the text.

Chapter Six

The Theme

Word the theme well.

A well-written title of a book is sometimes the greatest factor in its sale. Always keep in mind the basic idea you feel God wants to communicate. Know the direction you want the people to go. Keep the theme in mind, and try to express it in the most concise way possible. You should always be able to give your theme in one short sentence.

Know your theme thoroughly.

You need to have a clear, definite, intelligent grasp of the subject. This is also the greatest key to overcoming "stage-fright", which is a fear brought on by a focus on self, compounded with a perceived lack of preparation.

Live the theme.

Let it take complete possession of you, then preach it. Don't preach something that you don't live yourself. If you seem to be getting a word to correct a problem in your own life, then maybe it's a word just for you. When we preach about things we are personally failing in, we will tend to become harsh and legalistic, or we may be too permissive, excusing sin instead of opposing it.

Be sure your theme is one that people can understand.

Do not preach over people's heads. That means, try to avoid using your whole vocabulary, and never assume that your listeners are all Bible scholars. Billy Graham was noted for preaching on a level that a nine-year-old could understand, even though he was a respected scholar who could intelligently converse with learned men. The "Living Bible" was written to put the language of the King James Bible on the level of a child. Admit it: sometimes you need to read it, especially to get something out of the book of Job, or the Song of Solomon.

As our government becomes more and more involved in education, we realize that our overall literacy levels will continue to decline. Therefore, you are forced to keep it simple, while seeking to motivate the people to greater literacy and intellectual pursuits.

Jesus was known for His analogies. He took the things people were familiar with in the physical world, and used them to give spiritual truth. Of course, He often veiled things in parables so that carnal people wouldn't follow Him. He appealed to the spirit and to the heart more than to the mind. Remember that our purpose is to bring people to God, not just sell them on the idea of heaven. Everyone wants to go to heaven, but most do not want to repent of their sins and live for Jesus.

Have a definite aim in the treatment of your theme.

Aim to hit something. Do not ramble. Your purpose is not to talk. It is to communicate a specific truth that is on the heart of God for this people. Take them someplace in particular. "Mark, aim, hit, and then see if it struck the target. Then fire again!" If you expect results, you are much more likely to get them.

Choose a theme in accord with your experience.

If you are sad, do not preach on "joy". Get into God's presence, become joyful, and then preach about it! Do not preach holiness if you are not living a holy life. Of course, since we are called to preach holiness, we need to pursue it with our whole hearts. On the same line, avoid preaching victory over sin if you are not enjoying a victorious life. An actor can play a role. A preacher should not. During the Middle Ages, actors were not regarded as honored icons of society as they are in our culture. The Greek term for actor was "hypocritos," or "one who wears a mask."

Make sure your theme is suitable to the time, place, and occasion or your message

Easter is an ideal time to preach on the resurrection of Christ. During the Christmas season, we are expected to preach on the birth of Christ. This is, of course, subject to the Holy Spirit's direction.

Gathering Sermon Material

Reading

What have I ever read on this subject? What do I have in the library that would be profitable or helpful? Does your church have a library? Do you have access to a good public library?

Keep in mind the direction of writing today. As our culture becomes more and more humanistic, the books available reflect those anti-Christian values. Modern history texts often omit all references to God and religion, and portray key Christian leaders as heathens. This is called "revisionist history." Fortunately, we have Christian historians who are digging out old documents and writing good books that reflect a more accurate version of history.

We should be aware of science. There are many wonderful illustrations of spiritual truth in science, but we must also be aware of "science falsely so-called," such as "Christian Science," and the "science" of evolution. Many writers of today have been thoroughly indoctrinated with the doctrine of evolution, and it infects all of their ideas.

Having said this, there is still value in having access to encyclopedias and libraries, especially if we are aware of the worldview of the writers. The more you read, the greater your resources for illustration. Also, rediscover the biographies of great Christians. They are more available now than ever, and are a great resource for spiritual growth.

Observation

What have I observed that will throw light on this subject? What are my own life experiences? A good preacher must have wide-open eyes and ears.

Jesus did. When he walked with His disciples beside a field being cultivated, He would point and say, "Behold a sower went forth to sow." He immediately had their full attention, especially when He led them to truths that they couldn't grasp without further explanation. When they looked at flowers, He would make an observation about grace, saying, "consider the lilies of the field, how they grow." He would then talk to them about their own growth.

Jesus spoke much about relationships, and the importance of honest confrontation. Have you seen the results of such action? Have you seen the results of gossip or slander? Have you ever talked about someone when you should have talked to him? Your past successes or failures in life can be your most valuable and penetrating sermon illustrations.

Meditation

Have I ever thought on this subject? Meditation is like a "clean" animal ruminating on food. He will swallow grass, and then bring it back up to chew it thoroughly. We should memorize key verses or passages of the Bible, and then meditate on them. That involves personalizing and visualizing. For instance, after you memorize Psalm 24, visualize everything on earth as God's property, and think of Him creating it all. Think of yourself ascending into the hill of the Lord and seeking Him with all of your heart, and imagine being with Jesus when He says, "Lift up your heads, o ye gates..."

Organization

What have I gathered on this subject?

A pitiable and deplorable sight is to see a minister fretting and fuming a day or two before the week-end about his sermon for the coming Sunday. Preserve the results of your reading, observation and meditation. Keep a file on subjects. Organize your accumulated materials by subject in a way that is most useful for your own study. Some possible headings are:

- Salvation.
- Holy Spirit.
- Doctrines.
- Character Qualities
- Bible Characters.

- Family and Relationships
- Christmas
- Easter
- Cults

Arranging Sermon Material

Organization is extremely important.
Some sermons are described in Genesis 1:2: "without form and void".

Advantages of arranging your sermon material.

The advantage of such organization to the preacher is that it gives him a clear grasp of the subject matter.

The advantage relative to the sermon is that it tends to make it more effective.

The advantage to the audience is that it is easy for them to follow.

Also, it facilitates the continuity of the theme throughout the message.

Characteristics of a Good Arrangement.

Thematic Consistency

A preacher should learn the importance of concentrating on one theme at a time. If you find yourself wandering to another central idea, come back to the track you were on.

Logical Cohesiveness

Divide the sermon so that it connects and is in sequence one with the other.
First the seed, then the blade, then the ear, then the full corn.
First the negative . . . then the positive;
First the abstract, then the concrete;
First the general, and then the particular.

Organizational Clarity

It is possible to verify the degree to which you have clearly organized your material. Generally, it can be said that the people should be able to some degree articulate what you just said after they have heard it. That is, those who have paid attention should be able to see a simple outline of your message in their mind, or at least in their sermon notes.

The Arrangement

The sermon needs an outline.

A sermon needs an outline just as the human body needs a skeleton. (Allegory) You not only need a theme and goal, but you need clearly defined steps along the way. The plan should be easy for the listeners to follow.

Example: Theme - **"How to become a Christian"**:

- ☐ Admit.
- ☐ Commit.
- ☐ Submit.
- ☐ Transmit.

Messages built with striking outlines are more easily remembered than rambling sermons. An arrangement is remembered by the preacher as well as by the congregation.

Assembling the Sermon

The Body of the Message

The "body" of the sermon is also called the "Plan" or "Argument". This is the presentation of the substance of your presentation. You stimulate interest, even curiosity, by a good introduction, and you reiterate the basic principles and call for a response in your conclusion.

The divisions, or sub-points, should be related, and should follow a logical sequence. In a topical sermon, the negative illustrations (problem) will normally come before the positive application of scripture (solution). Negatives in general are dealt with in the early part of any persuasive discourse. Always leave the people with hope and faith.

There is no inherent beauty in a skeleton. The beauty comes from the illustrations, elaborations, and applications added by the preacher. It is also affected by the style of the speaker, and the related logistics. The division should be set forth in a full, definite and clear manner. The division should be natural and logical in their order from one to another. The transition from one point to the next should be clear, but not so abrupt that the audience is lost along the way.

The Divisions.

What?

What are you talking about? Define your subject. Give clear explanations concerning the times, culture, geography, or whatever information that will set the scene and help the listeners form pictures in their imagination. Use contrasts, comparisons, and illustrations. "All illustration is to a sermon what a window is to a building -- that which lets light in."

Who?

What are the main characters involved. What are the character qualities of the "heroes," and what are the faults of the "villeins." What insights do we have into their lives, and what can we learn from their mistakes or triumphs?

Why?

Why is it true? Why should I believe and accept it? Why should I be sitting here listening to you? What does this story have to do with me? Begin your argument by using some fact already known to the hearer, and always give them fresh and pertinent information that means something to them.

How?

Show how points one and two are brought about. How does it take place? How did the events and circumstances lead up to this, and how could it affect my own life?

What Then?

What should I do in response to this message? For example, in I Corinthians 15, Paul gave a great and detailed word on the end times and the resurrection. He concludes with a "therefore."

> *"Therefore, my beloved brethren, be ye stedfast, unmoveable, always abounding in the work of the Lord, forasmuch as ye know that your labour is not in vain in the Lord."* [62]

Peter also did this. He set the scene for and end-times holocaust, and then gave a rhetorical question:

> **"Seeing then that all these things shall be dissolved, what manner of persons ought**

---
[62] 1 Corinthians 15:58

ye to be in all holy conversation and godliness...[63]

Generally, the sermons of scripture all have such a definable purpose. They often begin with an introduction which establishes the credentials of the author ("Paul, an apostle of God.. not by the will of man..."), affirms the relationship of the writer to the hearer ("... to Timothy, my own son in the faith..."), and then describe the situations faced by the objects of the letters. The conclusion (or application) is often signaled by a "therefore..." In fact, a good rule of thumb for expositors:

"Whenever you see a 'therefore', find out what it is there for."

In the first division -- What is it? by explanation;
In the second division -- Who did it? by examination;
In the third division -- Why is it? by argumentation;
In the fourth division -- How . . . by what means.
And the fifth answers the question, "What Then" . . . by application.

Application

Instruction
What should I do about the teaching I have just heard?

Persuasion
Why should I feel deeply about it?
Why should I choose to act on the Word?

Motivation
Get the person to act on his aroused feeling toward God.

The Conclusion

Make it short (three to five minutes). If you say, "And now finally . . ." then let it be finally! Avoid using the old excuse that Paul said "finally" several times in Philippians. Some people wake

---

[63] II Peter 3:11

up on the cue of an "in conclusion" from the preacher, and may get something out of the sermon after all. Leave your congregation longing, not loathing.

Chapter Seven

Types of Sermons

1. Running Commentary

This involves going through a passage of scripture, alternately reading and expounding on the text. It may be a detailed analysis, or an overview of a large segment of the Bible. Keep in mind that much of the Bible is, in essence, a series of sermons in and of itself. In fact, some church services have been very effective with just a reading of the Bible without added commentary. But this is rare. Generally, people need some amplification, illustration, and practical application. Sadly, our average literacy level is much lower than it was two hundred years ago, and people need things spelled out in simple terms.

Chrysostom

"Even when severely rebuking, when blazing with indignation, he never seems alien, never stands aloof, but throws himself in among them, in a very transport of desire to check, and rescue, and save. Is there, indeed, any preacher, ancient or modern, who in these respects equals John Chrysostom?

> " ... The early Christians disliked to hear, or make, a smoothly symmetrical and elegantly finished oration, like those of the secular orators. They wished for more familiar and free addresses, such as we call a prayer-meeting "talk"; and this was precisely the meaning of their words "homily" and "sermon". The preacher took up his passage of scripture - usually somewhat extended - in a familiar way, sentence by sentence, with explanations and remarks, as he saw occasion; sometimes we find Chrysostom actually returning to go over the passage again, that it may suggest further remarks. At length, he would be apt to seize upon some topic of doctrine or practice which the text had directly or indirectly suggested, and discuss

that by way of conclusion, not infrequently wandering off into the thoughts which one after another occurred." [64]

Martin Luther

He was a great exponent of this style: "He never used much in the way of formal outline, but was strong on explanation, argument, illustration, imagination, application."

Today

This style is becoming popular again. The important thing is to avoid superficiality. Get to the substance of the text, and try to be consistent with the intent of the original author. This can only be done by being very familiar, not only with the text, but also with the context. (Note again the five things Luther was "strong" on.)

2. Structured Exposition

Structural exposition involves a formal and somewhat detailed outline, along with brief notes where needed. One of the first, and one of the greatest, to use this method was Matthew Henry. (See next example.) The method gradually became more structured, and more balanced in the shape of the outline (see example # Two below). This style reached its fullest development by the middle of this century, but seems now to be undergoing a decline. It can become too dry, and seem artificial.

Example 1 - (from Matthew Henry's Commentary)

Psalm 57:7-11

1. Introductory remarks.
2. How he prepares himself for the duty of praise (vs. 7)
   a. With reference to God's providence.
   b. With reference to the worship of God.
3. How he excites himself to the duty of praise (vs. 8)
   Explanations and comment.

---

[64] <u>Post-Nicene Father</u>, vol. 13; pg. iv; emphasis mine

4. How he prides himself in the work of praise (vs. 9)
   a. His own heart was enlarged in praising God.
   b. He desired to bring others to praise God.
5. How he furnishes himself with matter for praise (vs. 10)
   Explanations and comment.
6. How he leaves it at last to God to glorify his own name (vs. 11)
   Comment and conclusion.

Note: This outline is partly formal, partly formless. It represents a stage in the development of a formal outline.

If a structured outline is going to be used at all, the modern tendency would be to give it more color and shape, thus ...

Example 2

Psalm 57:7-11:4

1 INTRODUCTION
   Here is an amazing thing: a man untroubled, although he is surrounded by "lions"! (vs. 4).
2 MY HEART IS STEADFAST ON EARTH (VS. 7)
   a The key is praise, which must be:
      1) Personal   (vs. 7)
      2) Prevenient   (vs. 8)
      3) Public   (vs. 9)
   b Such praise is possible only when you can affirm of God that:
3 THY LOVE IS STEADFAST IN HEAVEN (vs. 10)
   a. Serenity comes from knowing that the love of God is:
      1) Powerful ("great to the heavens").
      2) Providential (His "clouds" symbolize abundance).
      3) Punctilious (He is "faithful").
4 CONCLUSION (vs. 11)
   A confident prayer, affirming God's triumph in heaven and on earth.

NOTE: Some would consider that outline too formal, or artificial, to represent David's passionate outpourings. Note also that it represents a thematic treatment of the passage (praise finding its source in love), rather than an exposition of what David actually said.

3. The Topical Sermon (also called a "thematic sermon")

The two most commonly used types, and the most basic, are the topical and the expository sermons. The topical sermon is built around one term or idea, and usually includes a number of different scriptural references related to that idea. For example, the topic may be general, such as: love, hope, faith, or salvation. It may also be more specific, such as the love of God, faith for healing, or redemption.

In using this method, we are taking a subject mentioned in scripture and discussing it on its own merits. A "topical concordance" is a virtual necessity for this. One of the first to use this method systematically was Jean Claude, a seventeenth century Frenchman.

A common way to prepare for a topical sermon is to begin by looking up related words in a concordance, and then studying the references in context. For example, if you want to teach on the topic of "depression," you would look up every reference to "cast down," "disquieted," "distressed," etc., and then look for antonyms such as "joy," "gladness," and see how they are achieved through the context.

Be careful to arrange the material in a logical and practical manner. Some preachers have been known to read several isolated verses from several texts without really developing the thought. It does not take sharp people long to detect that he has been writing down a list straight from the concordance. Remember that just because some scriptures use the same word does not mean that they are necessarily on the same topic.

After looking for related terms in scripture, begin to look for related stories in the Bible and from history. Stick with the theme, and remember: never mix analogies or metaphors. That creates confusion.

4. Life Situations

This sermon finds its origin in some current incident, or, it may draw upon a current problem facing the people. It has the advantage of usually capturing the people's attention easily, because it involves something about which they are already thinking. For example, if there is a flood or earthquake, you can use that to get the people thinking about the end times, or about the Biblical purposes of catastrophes. You can talk about "when the enemy comes in like a flood..." and the people will quickly relate to it.

On the day of Pentecost, the people in Jerusalem were amazed at the way the Christians talked and acted. Peter led them immediately from what they were seeing to the Word. *"This is that spoken of by the prophet Joel..."* (Acts 2:16) When Paul was in Athens on Mars Hill, he noticed the monument inscribed to *"The Unknown God."* He made that monument the focal point of his illustrated sermon. (Acts 17:23)

The problem with life situation sermons is the temptation to preach about some topic about which you have just been privately counseling. If some couple is having financial problems, you might think, "Say, there's a lot of folks who need to hear this counsel." But if people hear their situation brought up in a sermon, or if they think they are being used as an unnamed illustration, they will easily become offended. If you find that a member of the church is seeing a psychiatrist, for heaven's sake do not get up the next Sunday and preach against psychiatrists. They will perceive that you are preaching at them, and will be defensive.

5. Biographical

This refers to a sermon built around one of the characters from the Bible, or around some Christian hero. The most popular sermon series are based on the lives of David, Moses, or Joseph, because there is so much detail given about them. As you go through the incidents in their lives, you will come to many vivid illustrations of truths that will teach us to correctly respond to God, to life, or to temptations. The important thing here is that you avoid laboring the obvious, but look for wisdom.

Example: When we read the story of Abigail, we see on the surface that she "saved the day" and appeased the anger of David and his men, thus averting bloodshed for Nabal's house, and gaining the admiration of David. She "became the bride" and lived happily ever after. But doesn't the Bible say that wives shouldn't speak evil of their husbands? Was Nabal unfair to David, or did he know what Saul had done to Abimelech and the priests who had helped David before? Abigail's disloyalty resulted in the sudden death of her husband, but she did not become "the bride" of David. She became a member of his harem. She was taken captive by the Amalekites, and her son was passed over later as an heir to the crown. Abigail is not a "type of the church."

6. Bible Readings

Definition: The reading of a number of passages of Scripture and their comparison one with another.

Advantages:

It is simpler than other forms of sermon development. This is good for a beginner in homiletics, because the Word of God does speak for itself to the spiritual hearer. A good example for such a reading is the Revelation, which includes a special blessing on the hearer. When you stick to reading, you are less likely to insert some of your goofy interpretations of the prophetic symbols and types.

This method can also help prevent mind-wandering, because the speaker stays directly with the text of scripture. It keeps the preacher Biblical, and generally helps prevent a one-sided view of the truths in the Bible.

The reading method helps keep your personal Bible reading current, because you must do some reading to determine what to read, and to practice it. In application, a "Bible reading" is much like a "dramatic reading," where attention is given to some level of dramatic interpretation. It won't work if you read with a monotone, or if you mispronounce words.

The Method

Find out the teaching of the whole Bible on the subject chosen. Examine and research related words, such as "faith . . . belief . . . trust..."

On your note pad, use various headings, and answer the questions a good news reporter must answer in a brief article: "what, who, why, how, and what then." Next, take the concordance, look up the word "faith", and write under each heading.

Example:
"Faith is the substance" -- What.
"Without faith it is impossible to please God" -- Why.
"Faith cometh by hearing" -- How.

CAUTION: Do not use too many texts.

7. The Textual Sermon.

In this method, the structure of the message is built on a Bible text. Of course, there should be a single dominating theme, but it is developed by expounding on the specific passage used as a text.

8. The Question and Answer Method.

The outline's main points are questions related to a theme. The time is spent clearly providing answers to the questions. As all news reporters know, the basic questions are: who, what, where, when, how, and why. In preaching, we generally add the question, what then, since we are not concerned with merely informing, but we are solidly in the business of persuading.

9. The Expository Sermon.

Definition: The textual and the topical sermons occupy themselves chiefly with some one certain thought or topic suggested by the text: while the expository sermon occupies itself with the exposition of the entire scripture chosen. This sermon begins with a text, and enlarges on the ideas presented by the writer.

The advantage of expository preaching.

It produces a biblical preacher and hearer. Ultimately, the purest preaching focuses on the Bible, and brings its timeless truths to the lives of the hearers without diluting the intent of the writers. The expository sermon draws its direction from the original message, rather than simply using scripture to develop a topical theme based on the speaker's study and observations.

Expository preaching also conforms to the biblical ideal of preaching. It was the method Stephen used in Acts 7-8. He did a general overview of the Pentateuch, showing that the culmination of Israel's history was the cross of Christ. While most of his listeners were less than favorable to his analysis, they would have to admit at least that he was preaching God's Word.

The Possible Disadvantages of Expository Preaching.

Monotony

An expository series may go on for several weeks or months on a subject or book One pastor, for instance, decided to preach a sermon on the tabernacle of Moses. By the time he finished his research and outlines, he had forty-six hours of teaching involved. It's advisable to keep an ear tuned to the Spirit, and an eye on the audience. Focus on what God is saying, and meet the needs of the people where they are. It is possible to maintain an expository series and still do that, but you have to be on the ball.

Laziness

The preacher may get so settled in with his expository series that he fails to seek the Lord for clear direction. He may think, "I have been preaching so long that I can get up with little preparation and talk off the top of my head." Good preaching is always work, and requires diligent preparation, both spiritually and academically.

Excessive Text for the Time Frame.

"Today, we're going to cover the Pentateuch." You may try to cover so much that people grasp little. It is usually better to focus on a single incident or character. You are not going to usually give people everything they will need for life in one sermon. You build on truth a little at a time, and seek to promote specific responses.'

Too Confining.

A detailed expository series commitment may keep you from dealing with current topics. Again, keep the specific and relevant needs of the people in mind. Your purpose is not to gather people to hear you preach. Your purpose in preaching is to change lives.

Suggestions for Expository Preaching

Choose a portion of scripture that contains one leading thought or theme.

There are many truths communicated in the Sermon on the Mount (Matthew 5-7). Matthew's account does not relate every word given by Jesus. It covers the main topics taught by Jesus in communicating the Kingdom of God. There are many individual sermons in this text, as there are in most chapters of the Bible.

Choose texts from different parts of the Bible.

Use short sections of scripture that reinforce the same basic principle. This will help the hearers see that you are not drawing strange conclusions from interpreting isolated verses, but that you are communicating broad-based principles reiterated by several of the anointed writers of the canon. Be careful that you avoid reading a series of verses just because they have a common word. If you do skip around with multiple texts, then you must make sure your line of reasoning is organized and easy to follow.

Do a thorough study of the entire text.

Understand every phrase. Research every significant word, especially if you do not know the meaning yourself. Look it up in your Hebrew/Greek dictionary. Examine it in context to see what the writer really meant by it. Study the story in context. Know the history and sociology that forms the setting. Good study is hard work.

Be practical.

Always apply the message to the situation and needs of the people. The Bible is relevant to us today, and it has the answers we need. Keep your basic purpose in mind when you preach and teach.

Conclusion

You may use any or all of these sermon types, but always remain true to yourself, to your own personality and style. Always seek to use the type of sermon that will most effectively communicate the truths you believe God wants to communicate to the people who hear you, and be sensitive to the prompting of the Holy Spirit.

****

PRACTICUM

☐ Find in a book, commentary, or reference Bible, an outline of the Twenty-Third Psalm, and copy it out. Always acknowledge the source of anything you copy, even if it is not word for word.

☐ Develop an outline of your own on the same Psalm.

****

John Wesley

How to Prepare an Expository Sermon

**Theme, Introduction, Development and Conclusion.
Qualities Requisite for Success as an Expositor**

Chapter Eight

How to Prepare an Expository Sermon

Preface:

Writers on the subject of preaching are unanimous in regard to the value of expository preaching. All agree that it is the most effective form of pulpit eloquence. Very few of our modern preachers are using this method. The reason for this seems to be either a lack of knowledge of the value of expository sermons, or a lack of ability in preparing them.

The Purpose of Expository Preaching

The expository sermon is an effort to explain, illustrate. and apply the scripture to the life of the listener. Expository preaching is the consecutive treatment of some book or extended portion of scripture on which the preacher has concentrated, head and heart, brain and brawn, over which he has thought and wept and prayed, until it has yielded up its inner secret and the spirit of it has passed into his. It is not based on the preposition: "What do I want to say, and where can I get some scriptural support for my idea?" Rather, it flows from the question, "What is God saying to me through His Word, the Bible?"

The Value of Expository Preaching

Expository preaching helps the hearers find in the sacred writings the true interpretation of life. This is both a high ideal and most delightful task, kindling in the soul of the preacher that spark of heavenly fire that glows with enthusiasm and conviction.

Phelps, in his "Theory of Preaching," says,

> "By parting with expository preaching, the pulpit has parted with its most important aid and stimulus to variety. No other one thing gives to preaching so wide a range of religious thought as the exposition of the Scriptures when it comes forth as the fruit of a rich, full mind -- rich in scholarly resources, and full of intense, practical aims."

Dean Brown, of Yale Divinity School, in the "Art of Preaching", declares:

> "I am a firm believer in the value of expository preaching."
> "It has the historic warrant of being apostolic."
> "It ensures a more thorough knowledge of the Bible on the part of the preacher himself."
> "Also develops a more thorough knowledge of the Bible on the part of the people."
> "It develops both in the pulpit and pew the Scriptural point of view, than which there is none better."

The habit of preaching expository sermons is a splendid disciple for the preacher. It gives him a more profound and vital interest in the study of the Bible. It encourages him to search there for sermon material rather than in the newspaper or in the works of science and philosophy. The notion that the Bible is not as interesting or as fruitful in sermonic material as these other fields is a gigantic mistake. The only reason that people think the Bible is uninteresting is because they do not know it.

The expository method also leads to a new method of studying the Scriptures. Instead of simply seeking the basis of sermons in individual texts, the expositor seeks to discover the meaning of a book or chapter. He is more like to view the Word of God from a larger perspective; and thus will be more likely to draw wisdom from his studies. This approach also helps the preacher maintain the mentality of a student, for he is more aware of the vast amount of truth he has yet to fully comprehend.

What Should a Preacher Know?

The one thing a preacher ought to know is his Bible; not only in the sense of an accumulation of texts, but also in the revelation of various statements to the context. The more he knows the Bible and endeavors to live it out in his own life, the better man he will be and the larger will be his ultimate influence on his people and community.

> The Church is suffering today from the ministrations of two types of men in the pulpit: those who are too broad, and those who are too narrow.

The "broad-minded" preacher is well informed about the Bible, but not involved in it. These people have lost their bearings and are trying to reach the popular mind by "lecturettes" on passing events. They can talk glibly about science or religion, or about culture and events, but they don't have a word from God. The Apostle Peter concluded his powerful discourse with an exhortation to *"grow in grace, and in the knowledge of our Lord and Saviour Jesus Christ."* [65] Note that he is not talking about knowledge about Jesus. He is talking about personal intimacy; a real relationship with the Lord. We are not just the promoters of the ideas of Jesus, we are "the ministers of Christ."

Secondly, there are some pulpiteers who are too "narrow". That is, their preaching is thoroughly orthodox and sincere, but they have poorly furnished minds. They have only a vague knowledge of the Bible as a whole. Their sermons lack depth of thought and are ineffective because they fail to relate Biblical truth to personal experience.

The Danger of "Harping on the Same String"

This is one of the dangers to which any preacher is liable to fall prey. He may be influenced in his preaching by his special lines of temperament, training or experience to focus too much on one kind of illustration, or on one idea.

Illustrations

If one preacher is a great fan of sports, he may use many sports-related illustrations, or even refer to his favorite teams ad nauseum. If one is given to imagination or heady philosophy, he is likely to spend much of his time in the clouds. He may spend too much time on theories and vague concepts and neglect the practical needs of the people. If one is affected with some physical ailment or having financial difficulties, his messages are likely to be somber and gloomy, or over-emphasize money in the meetings. If a church splits apart, then both factions will tend to overemphasize their side of the differences, and keep on preaching to the group that is no longer there.

---

[65] II Peter 3:18

Variety

The Lord did not make the flowers all of one kind. Neither did He ordain that the fruit should be all the same shape, size, color or taste. All the dangers of temperament, training and experience may in some measure be offset, however, when by the expository method we make the experience fit the truths of scripture rather than use the scripture to illustrate our own experience, as is likely to be the case in the topical method of preaching.

Love

The important thing to realize here is that the preacher should focus first on God and what He is saying, and secondly on the people, and what they are needing. That was the secret to the success of Jesus. He never did anything for a selfish purpose. Jesus did nothing to promote His career, reputation, or finances. He came only to do the will of the Father, and to help people.

Notice that Jesus, whose earthly family background was carpentry, used illustrations that related to farming or fishing. He was using frames of reference familiar to his people, such as the fishermen who were his closest disciples. Even when He was dying on the torturous cross, He expressed concern for Mary's needs, so He delegated to John the responsibility of taking care of her. The people could sense His purely unselfish motive, and were drawn to His ministry.

The Benefits of Expository Preaching for the Preacher

The expository method controls the preacher's religious outlook. This approach to the task of preaching tends to diminish the waste of time and loss of nervous energy to get a sermon, especially when you are engaged in a sermon series. Some preachers may fear that if they preach an extended series, such as a three-month series on the book of Romans, that they will be repetitious or boring. Actually, they will tend to give the people a greater variety of insights, because they are building on a practical and anointed discourse that deals with many needs in the church and home. In fact, the preacher who is searching for a last-minute word every week with no long-range plan will be far more likely to be repetitious, and less likely to focus on the real needs of the people.

Brown's Experience.

Brown spent one or two hours daily in the intensive study of individual books of the Bible. After the first four months of his ministry, he never spent even a quarter of an hour hunting for a text or a theme. "No other study" the same writer declares, "is so prolific of the finest quality and variety of homiletic material as the study of the Scriptures."

No other materials work into the realities of human life and the emergencies of men's souls so deftly as the materials thus gained. Once full of them, and with a mind assimilated to their quality, with a speech that holds them at the tongue's end, a preacher need never exhaust himself. He need never rack his brain, or roam the streets for something to say. The stream is perennial. It is the river of the water of Life.

It is uplifting of the mind "into a Biblical atmosphere, especially an atmosphere of faith in God and in this world's future."

It makes it easy to introduce topics that are not as easily welcomed in the minds of the listeners. (Finances, missions, marriage, women's public ministry, etc.)

The Benefits of Expository Preaching for Congregations

Expository preaching awakens an interest in the study of the Scriptures if the speaker effectively shows that the Bible provides practical answers to the problems of life. Nothing is more needed in our day than an awakened interest in the Bible. Many of the preachers today rely on a clever thought or even a catchy phrase to establish their sermon for the week. They commonly fail to get the listeners into the Word, largely because they themselves have not been "in the Word."

Science and literature have their value for the intellectual and esthetic natures, but the moral and spiritual, which are the most important, have their stimulus through contact with divine truth. The Bible is uniquely the book written to the spirit of man, not just to the intellect. That is why even brilliant unsaved scholars are unable to grasp its truths in context, and sincere believers can be blessed by it even if they do not fully understand every passage.

The sad thing about this age of education in which we live is that people do not know the most helpful and most interesting book in the world. For human interest and practical value, Shakespeare, Milton, and Tennyson, Longfellow and Lowell are not even close competition.

What a feeling of satisfaction and delight comes to a person who, after a sermon says: "I never heard it explained that way before." The experience is the starting point for renewed interest in the study of the Bible. Our objective is not just to impress people with the truths we see in scripture, but also to inspire people with a greater desire to study it themselves.

Reasons for Scarcity

Some people have heard many mediocre sermons.

Poor exposition in part has led to the idea that Biblical expositions are dry and uninteresting. People attending church are not desperately anxious to discover what happened to the Jebusites. The preacher must start with the auditor's vital need, and throw all the light he can on that. In other words, it is up to the preacher to captivate the attention of the listeners by showing them that the message relates precisely to their world, and to their personal needs.

Some people do not understand what an expository sermon really is.

It is not a running, skittering comment, suited to a Sunday school class. It is not a prayer meeting style of comment full of pious homily, and with a certain amount of loose exegesis. It is not an exhaustive digest of all the commentaries to which one has access. If an exposition is going to be effective, there must be unity in the message, progress in the content, organization in the material, and a definite goal overall.

Some people do not seem to be seeking expository sermons.

There is a feeling that the demand for popular preaching, and the adapting of the message to present-day problems, makes expository preaching difficult. The Bible is a vital, as stirring and as thrilling when properly applied as ever it was. There is no realm of human thought or activity in which the Scriptures cannot be applied. For every relationship in life in the home, the community and the nation, at school, at business or at play, the Bible sets forth principles to meet every need and solve every problem.

Some preachers have difficulties in preparing or delivering discourses of this type.

Successful work in exposition requires a keen exegetical or analytical mind, with ability to get into the spirit of the writer and express with conviction and enthusiasm the applications of the text.

This combination of spirit, intellect and emotion is not a common one, but where

> they are combined in the same person
> there is expository power.

There is no more vitalizing force, no impulse more quickening to the soul, than the discovery in the Bible itself of the interpretation and meaning of life. To give utterance to these discoveries to a waiting world is one of the richest experiences of the human soul. Any preacher would do well to seek it.

Do you get the impression that Pastor Totman's vacation was just a little too long?

Speaking as an Oracle of God.

> *"As every man hath received the gift, even so minister the same one to another, as good stewards of the manifold grace of God. If any man speak, let him speak as the oracles of God; if any man minister, let him do it as of the ability which God giveth: that God in all things may be glorified through Jesus Christ."* [66]

---

[66] I Peter 4:10-11

There are many pulpits today being filled by unregenerate or carnal men and women who are in the clergy because they want to voice their opinions. They will use the Bible to support their ideas when they can. But the purpose of a true Christian preacher is not to use the Bible to express himself. His purpose is to hear what God is saying by the Spirit and through the Word, and be a faithful messenger. The ideas that originate in our minds, no matter how noble our brilliant they may sound, are ultimately foolish. God does not need smart people to sit on His board of directors. God needs people who can take orders without question and convey messages without alteration.

The Bible is logical and intelligent, but the first appeal is to the spirit of the spiritual man. People who are not saved are spiritually dead, and therefore spiritually blind and deaf. They can relate only to the physical and psychological side of life.[67] In fact, they can only really hear and receive the message of salvation if the Holy Spirit touches them with convicting power. Only God can open their eyes to spiritual reality. Good preaching will point people to Jesus, but the work of regeneration is always supernatural.

The true pastor must always keep in mind that he is discipling people to Jesus, and not to himself. A successful preacher must always battle the temptation to build a church as a monument to himself. So also the expositor must always keep in mind that he is above everything else a messenger for the Head of the Church. He must not focus on "what will the people think of me," but "What is God saying to the church today," and secondly, "what do the people need?"

> *"Let a man so account of us, as of the ministers of Christ, and stewards of the mysteries of God."* [68]

A steward is a servant who takes care of that which belongs to his master. Paul told the Corinthians that we are not only servants of Jesus, but that we are stewards of the mysteries of God. God will hold us accountable for not only the way we relate to His people, but also

---

[67] ref. I Corinthians 2:14
[68] I Corinthians 4:1

for how we have faithfully handled His Word. Being a consistent expository preacher is good stewardship.

The constant danger in preaching is pride. As soon as a preacher gains the confidence of people as a spiritual leader, he is tempted to take the honor of an office to himself. People are naturally "king-makers". When the children of Israel were carnal, they wanted a king. They did not want to relate to God as their King, because the carnal mind likes to focus on something physical. The people cried out for a king, and God gave them Saul. He was just what they wanted. He was even humble, until the pressures of success got to him, and he took himself too seriously. He got the position of king, and the people were all too willing to make him wealthy and powerful. Of course, the wealth did not destroy him. The pride did.

There are two great hindrances to hearing from God: pride, and moral impurity. God *"resists the proud, but gives grace to the humble."*,[69] If you do a word study in the scriptures, you might discover that grace means much more than "unmerited favor." It also relates to supernatural impartation of power. Grace is God's ability working through human vessels. Pride causes us to focus on self. Humility makes us keenly aware that without Jesus, we can do nothing. [70]We are dependent on God in the ministry, but we *"can do all things through Christ who strengthens (us)"*.[71]

Moral impurity also hinders our ability to hear spiritually. God told Jeremiah, *"If thou take forth the precious from the vile, thou shalt be as my mouth."* [72] Jeremiah prophesied in Judah, just before the great conquest and captivity by Babylon. Jerusalem was full of "prosperity" preachers, who prophesied blessing and deliverance for Judah, just as they had seen one hundred and thirty-six years earlier when the Assyrians had tried to destroy them. But Jeremiah was the prophet of doom. He told the people to prepare for captivity, because God had raised up Nebuchadnezzar as His rod of correction. While the other preachers were popular and successful, Jeremiah suffered. But he spoke as God's voice, even though he was never well received

---

[69] I Peter 5:5
[70] John 15:5
[71] From Philippeans 4:13
[72] Jeremiah 15:19

by the people. He was God's oracle to God's people, and he was faithful.

A Living Testimony

Shortly before his death, Dr. F. B. Meyer, on the occasion of a visit to Liverpool, recalled an incident that marked a point of vital interest and importance in his development as a preacher. Referring to the days when he began his ministry in that city, he said: "I can never forget the spot where we stood together one Sunday evening after Mr. Birrell had heard me preach at Pembroke Chapel, 'That was a good sermon' he said, 'but it was on a topic which journalists can handle better than we can. If you are going to that line, you will come to the end of your resources. Be advised by me, and be content with the golden stores of Scripture, and you will never be wanting either the subject of a sermon or the congregation'". "That" said Dr. Meyer, "changed my life. I have been content to unfold the wealth of Scripture. All the books I have written and fifty-seven years of preaching find me only at the beginning of realizing the literary beauty, the historic interest, the profound moral and spiritual charm of the Old Bible."

The Expository Sermon Outline   **(Briefest form)**

- Introduction.
- Development.
- Conclusion.

The Sermon Outline   **(More elaborate form)**

1. Text.
2. Explanation.
3. Introduction.
4. Proposition.
5. Division
6. Development.
7. Conclusion.

The Sermon Outline**(Expository form)**

1. Theme.
2. Scripture.
3. Introduction.
4. Division.
5. Development.
6. Conclusion

Sample of an Expository Outline

Theme: "The Believer's Walk"
Text   Colossians 1:9-12

9. *"For this cause we also, since the day we heard it, do not cease to pray for you, and to desire that ye might be filled with the knowledge of his will in all wisdom and spiritual understanding;*
10. *That ye might walk worthy of the Lord unto all pleasing, being fruitful in every good work, and increasing in the knowledge of God;*
11. *Strengthened with all might, according to his glorious power, unto all patience and longsuffering with joyfulness;*

12. Giving thanks unto the Father, which hath made us meet to be partakers of the inheritance of the saints in light:

Introduction

The Christian life is not focused on a personal evangelistic experience, but on a vital and living relationship with God through the Lord Jesus Christ. God gives us "paths to dwell in." (Isaiah 58:12) The life of the Christian is a walk, because it is an ongoing, dynamic, and progressive lifestyle that prepares us for eternity.

Division and Development

A. The **nature** of the walk.
1. Worthy of the Lord (vs. 10).
2. According to the revealed will of God (vs. 9).

B. The **motive** of the walk.
1. Unto the Lord; i.e. The Lord Himself (vs. 10).
2. Not self-centered, or self-sufficient.

C. The **means** of the walk
1. Faith in Christ -- the beginning (vs. 4).
2. Prayer -- continued by (vs. 9).
3. The Word of God -- source of knowledge of God's will (vs. 9).
4. Indwelling Spirit of God (vs. 4)

D. The **results** of the walk.
1. Well-pleasing to God (vs. 10).
2. Truthful in every good work (vs. 10).
3. An increasing knowledge of God (vs. 10).
4. Spiritual graces:
   a. Patience.   b. Long-suffering.
   c. Joy.   d. Thankfulness.
5. An inheritance with the saints in light (vs. 11 and 12)

Conclusion

"For ye were sometimes darkness, but now are ye light in the Lord: walk as children of light..." (Ephesians 5:8)

Distinctions in the Expository Form

The form of the outline given is the same for all kinds of sermons. The expository type has two primary distinctions:

- ❏ It usually takes a larger portion of Scripture for its foundation.
- ❏ The development of the discourse is always an exposition and application of the Scripture selected.

An expository sermon has:
- ↬ Explanation
- ↬ Exposition
- ↬ Application

Example

Text. *"Without faith it is impossible to please God."* [73]

Explanation	1.	What is faith?
	2.	What is the nature of God?
Exposition	3.	What does the Bible say about faith?
Application	4.	Why it is impossible to please God without faith?
	5.	How can I please God?

To make it clearer, the form might be changed to the following outline:
- ♦ Getting the idea from the Scripture.
- ♦ Securing a contact of the theme with the needs or interests of the people.
- ♦ Giving an exposition of the package involved.
- ♦ Making the application.

For an expository sermon to be a success the theme selected must relate to the lives of the listeners, the Scripture explained must show broad and intensive study, and the application must be such that the hearers not only understand the theoretical meanings, but also their practical bearings on life. If these principles are applied, the message should receive a good hearing, and the preparation and delivery of sermons will become an increasing joy. He who can interpret the meaning of the Scriptures in

---

[73] Hebrews 11:6

terms of modern experience will never be without an audience, and he will have the additional satisfaction of giving to the people knowledge that will make them "wise unto salvation through faith which is in Christ Jesus."

The passage selected for an expository sermon may range from one verse to an entire short book of the Bible. Keep in mind that the scope is that the sermon must be a cohesive unit of thought. It must hold together in a logical progression of ideas leading to a definite Biblical conclusion. Also, the expositor should not read vague or confusing passages without explanation. Sometimes it is necessary for the sake of brevity to give a summary of the background, rather than read the entire passage related to the scene in focus.

Whole Book

Short Book Exposition
Example: Philemon.

This letter, usually read in its entirety, sets forth Paul's method for dealing with personal conflicts, and is capable of a very practical application. In this personal correspondence, the Apostle Paul asked Philemon to receive Onesimus "no longer as a servant, but more than a servant, a brother beloved"; to receive him as he would receive Paul himself. He further declares that if there is a financial consideration involved in setting his slave free, to "put that to my account . . . I will repay it."

Now, slavery is a thing of the past. But here is the point. Paul asked one man to surrender his personal freedom when faith demanded it, and return to his master. Of his friend, he asked the surrender of his social privileges and to receive his slave as a brother, because of his faith. He was making a demand of each of these men on the basis of their faith in Christ that went to the limit. He set before them the ideal of a brotherhood that overruled all social and financial considerations, and in the principles Paul here as he lays them down, we have the only true remedy for all the industrial and social ills of modern society.

When you take any short book, either an epistle or one of the minor prophets, you will need to do your homework and know as much as possible about the author, the circumstances surrounding the writing, the social setting, and the purpose of the writing. Generally, this will take more work than the thematic analysis. Your purpose as an expositor is to communicate the heart of the message according to the intent of the original writer, and then to apply the unchanging principles to present day life.

Long Book Exposition

If you are doing expository preaching on a longer book, you will generally do so in a series. These series can take many months if done well, without losing the interest of the listeners. Of course, to keep people coming back, you will need to avoid being repetitious, or superficial. You will also need to keep your audience in mind, and avoid getting so bogged down in academic details that you miss the practical application, or the personal aspects. The Bible generally gives us enough information about characters that we can find many interesting personal stories to tell. We can also see ourselves in the people involved.

Occasionally, you might do a survey series, in which you give a general overview. The temptation is to try to cover each story, one after another. In doing so, you will cover too much ground, and find yourself in too many topics to hold sustained interest. Try to grasp and communicate with a broad brush, and find out the essence of the overall message.

For example, the book of Judges is full of fascinating accounts of heroes like Samson and Gideon. Each story is rich with sermon material. The book can make for a great series. But if you want to cover the book in one message, you will need to look for the practical truth that permeates the whole period of the judges. This historical record gives us a vivid account of national life in a nation with no clearly defined leadership. The theme is "every man did that which was right in his own eyes." The people were constantly subject to oppression and bondage, because they all did their own thing. When they followed a self-seeking ambitious leader, they were still in trouble. On the other hand, every time God raised up a leader who had a servant's heart and was submitted to God, the people were successful and free. God leads through leaders whom He appoints and anoints.

Chapter Exposition

Many of the Psalms express one primary emotion, which easily becomes the theme for exposition. Dr. Chapman thus explains the twenty-third Psalm. He used it to emphasize the author's idea of possession. Thus: *"The Lord is **my** shepherd," "He maketh **me** lie down in green pastures, He restoreth **my** soul,"* and so on. The plan thus followed was to develop only one line of thought running through it.

Some of the Psalms even note in the introduction the event which prompted its writing, such as Psalm 51, the classic repentance chapter. It was David's response to the Prophet Nathan's rebuke for his adultery and murder. Psalm 34 was written after David made the mistake of going to Goliath's home town when fleeing from King Saul. He quickly realized that he was not at all popular with the Philistines. But God gave him a word of wisdom. He began to act like a demon-possessed man. Apparently, these heathens had executed demoniacs before, and had found that the demons leave the dead man and enter into other people in the room. They were afraid to kill him, so they just let him go.

When the people are given the background, then it is easier for them to get interested in the message of the text. Most of the 1,189 chapters in the Bible have a prominent truth to communicate, and make excellent units for expository study.

Short Passage Exposition

When using a single verse, an expository sermon is likely to be the explanation of the most significant words, and then the general meaning of the passage as intended by the writer. For example: Romans 1:16. *"The Gospel is the power of God unto salvation to everyone that believeth."* Here we have "Gospel" *(euaggelion)*, meaning "glad tidings" or "good news" the "power" *(Dunamis)*, meaning the dynamic power of God, or "unto salvation," which opens up a still large field. "Salvation" does not just mean, "ticket to heaven," as some might imply. *"Sodzo"* means "to heal, to make whole." The gospel is not just able to save us from hell, but it is for believers, to bring them to spiritual, mental, and physical wholeness. The power of the gospel saves us from sin.

WARNING It is a mistake, to think that the expository method requires discussing every subject in a book of a chapter, even when the studies are given consecutively. Remember that you are not producing a commentary. You are preparing a sermon upon a given subject and you choose that which is related to it.

Some preachers seem to imagine that in a series of expository sermons it is necessary for them to treat every chapter successively, or to prepare several sermons on the same chapter. Unless they are very highly gifted, and men of unusual spiritual power, this will become wearisome for the listeners.

Exposition means using the Scriptures in such a way as to select materials that have practical and vital interest, and can be applied with force and power. Furthermore, it only means choosing as much scripture for each discourse as is necessary for the development of the theme.

QUALITIES REQUISITE FOR SUCCESS AS AN EXPOSITOR

A Good General Education

A man with an untrained mind may give a good hortatory (emotional, devotional) discourse, but it is practically impossible for him to preach expository sermons.

A preacher with a good general education will benefit from his training in literature which will give him an appreciation of the best thought and its expression. We certainly do not agree with humanist philosophers such as Plato, Nietche, Voltaire, or Horace Mann, but we need to be aware of their false ideas. They have influenced the minds of people we deal with, and we need to understand their mindset in order to lead them to God's wisdom.

The man of God will receive much help from the study of logic, which will enable him to balance arguments and to present his thoughts in an orderly way. While the Christian faith is based on faith and not logic, it is indeed logical, especially from the perspective of the spirit.

A diligent preacher will be helped by the languages, especially the Greek, which will reveal to him the fine shades of meaning of the words used by Christ and the Apostles. In fact, a poor command of his own language will hinder his ability to communicate, and will tend to alienate the more literate of his constituency. The mastery of the English language, both in word usage and grammatical structure, is essential for the preacher who would seek to have a broad scope of influence.

His knowledge of history will enable him to understand the New Testament in its setting in world events. Also, all of history is "His Story." The more honest scholars view the events of people and nations, the more clearly they see that their response to God and His people is the single greatest factor in the rise and fall of any nation. A strong example is the island of Haiti. It was once a thriving and prosperous nation. But in the 1830s the nation turned away from Christianity. Haiti was officially dedicated to voodoo. Today, it remains one of the poorest and most dangerous countries on earth, in spite of its excellent natural resources.

Studies in psychology will show the preacher how men have tried to solve the ultimate problems of life and have failed. There is a danger in exploring this field under secular teachers, for the secular mind sees man as physical and psychological only, with no understanding of the reality of spirit.

But, all things considered, a broad education will better equip the man of God to reach people, especially literate ones. Gone are the days when ignorance was considered to be an indication of spirituality, or when poor technique was thought to be a mark of sincerity.

Bible Training

It really goes without saying that any preacher must know the Word of God. The more intimately we are acquainted with the characters, events, and ideas presented in these sixty-six sublime books, the more equipped we are to declare accurately that which God is saying today. The Bible is our greatest source for wisdom, sermon illustrations, and ideas. It should be our only source for sermon texts. It is impossible to be a preacher of God without being a preacher of the Bible.

Good Study Habits

One who attempts exposition and does not apply himself to study with sufficient industry and concentration is most surely headed for failure. Expository sermons cannot be produced on Saturday for the pulpit on Sunday. It takes time and effort to develop any good sermon.

You must meditate on the theme to be developed, and on the Scriptures you are seeking to communicate. You must also be aware of the meanings of words in the text, and the stories of the Word in context. The goal is to get into the mind and spirit of the writer, and that takes work.

Dr. Meyers said: "The highest point of sermon utterance is when a preacher is 'possessed', and certainly, in the judgment of the writer, such possession comes oftenest and easiest to a man who has lived, slept, walked and eaten in fellowship with a passage for the best part of a week."

Intense and Consistent Prayer

The greatest prerequisite for an effective preacher is prayer. Prayer is not a tool to bend God to our will and purpose. Real prayer is communion as well as communication with God, who already knows our needs and thoughts. Prayer brings us into to place where we can hear His voice, and respond to His will. The more we pray in faith and humility, the more we can expect God to work for us and through us. Ultimately, it is the Holy Spirit who does the work in the lives of the people. The preacher points to Jesus, but the healing and transforming is done by the Lord.

Oratorical Skill

This is the ability to take the idea involved in a passage of scripture and express its meaning and application with such persuasiveness and enthusiasm that the hearers will respond. It's not just what you say that matters. It is also how you say it. Preachers who carry the sublime truths of Scripture should be the most articulate and interesting speakers in the world, for they are speaking the clearest wisdom and most important thoughts in humanity.

The public declaration of God's Word is one of the greatest privileges given to any man or woman. The accomplishment of that task with power and skill is one of the greatest thrills we can know.

Don't bug me. I've been ministering in the flesh all day, and I'm zonked.

Vocal Expression and the Expository Method

Variety in Vocal Expression

One of the essential qualities of interesting speech is variety. Those who are new to preaching may have a tendency to become monotonous. Shouting and flailing can be monotonous if there is little or no variety in tone, pitch, or volume.

Many people think that they must adopt an entirely different and unnatural tone in the pulpit. Their nose rises a bit higher, their voice gets lower, and their demeanor becomes stiff and pretentious. Some even insist on speaking in "thee" and "thou" terms, as if seventeenth century vernacular were somehow the language of the Spirit.

The conversational style of speech is becoming the method of great preachers and orators. It wears better than any other kind of speech. It is said to be the method used by the great parliamentary speakers of England. The best preacher is really the best talker. Our goal is not to impress people with our oratory, but to move them with the Word of God. We want them to be inspired by Jesus, not impressed by our flesh.

A conversational style is the most interesting and effective preaching method, because it is easy for the congregation to relate and respond. A good rule of thumb is to speak to a crowd as if you were speaking to an individual. You must be friendly, honest, and sincere. Your goal is to overcome their mental roadblocks in order to lead them to the conclusion you have already drawn through your prayer and study in the Word.

In a conversation, you may become excited at times, but you do not need to shout. You may gesture for emphasis, but you should never pace around like a polar bear at the zoo. You drop your voice and lean forward when it is appropriate, but only to make the point more effectively.

"Soul"

The true oratory begins with the man. It is the expression of that which is in his soul. Intensity in public utterance, if it is not artificial, is only possible when the man himself is deeply stirred. We know that the soul of man is his mind, will, and emotion. While great preaching focuses on the spirit, it is communicated with soul. As one old preacher expressed it, "You can't go on feelings, but praise God you can feels what you're goin' on." The preacher's power in the pulpit will be proportionate to the extent to which his message has become a part of himself.

The pulpit is lacking in great preachers today because it is lacking in men of strong conviction. It is true, however, that the outstanding men of our time, as in all times, are the men who have no misgivings about the inspiration of the Scriptures, the deity of Christ or the reality of heaven and hell. Dr. F. D. Meyer's definition of an expository sermon is one on "An extended portion of Scripture on which the preacher has concentrated head and heart, brain and brawn, over which he has thought and wept and prayed, until it has yielded up its inner secret, and the spirit of it has passed into his spirit." No other type of sermon makes such a demand. It is this that develops conviction, enthusiasm, and enables one to speak with authority on the deep things of life.

How can a preacher become absorbed in his theme?

F. D. Meyer says that "probably on Sunday night, when the family has dispersed, he will take his Bible in hand and turn to the paragraph next in order to that from which he has preached during the day. The emotions that have wrought within his soul have not died down." He does this while he is still feeling the thrill of his message, and scans "the paragraph next in order until probably its valiant features, its lesson, or its pivotal sentences, grip him.". He then makes a few rough notes, "the fugitive thoughts, with footstep, light as a fairy's that may flit across his soul." "Next he investigates the original text, and then places it in the perspective of the entire book. Then he turns to commentaries and sermons; they set us thinking." The main preparation, however, is the reading and re-reading of the Biblical text.

Another great expositor tells us that he will read a given book, which he has set himself to expound, some ten or twenty times through, that he may catch the spirit of the author, and become steeped in his ruling motive and purpose. It is this method of preparing the sermon that makes the man and his message identical, so that when he preaches his style is natural, his words are spirit and life, and that which comes through his lips comes from his soul. In this way soul and speech combine, and the most effective speech is the inevitable result.

Chapter Nine

Sermon Divisions

The Theme

The appeal of the theme itself is determined by the temperament of the preacher. the needs of the congregation as he understands them, the pastor's experience, and his understanding of the Scriptures. The effective preacher will take the truths of God's Word and communicate them to the people in an interesting and response provoking way. His personality, experience, and communication skills is the link between the infallible Word and imperfect people.

Illustration from the Gospel of John.

Before beginning the study of any book of the Bible, you will need to study the critical questions dealt with in the text. The study of *logos* might be an interesting exercise in Greek and in philosophy. You might also read Fisher's "Grounds for Theistic and Christian Belief."

It is usually a good idea to read the introduction to the book itself in any critical commentary. Your enthusiasm, however, is to be found in the study of the Scriptures themselves, and not in essays or books about the Scriptures. Consider an English major. He will become an expert on Shakespeare, Milton, Tennyson, or any other poet, by reading their works, not just by reading critical dissertations about them.

First, study the book, with a focus on its general background and purpose. The first resource is what the author himself says. For example, look at John 20:31. The apostle said, *"But these are written, that ye might believe that Jesus is the Christ, the Son of God, and that believing ye might have life through his name*

We ought to know about John's close personal association with Jesus.. He was one of the "inner circle" -- one of those who understood Him best. John had the grace gift of "mercy." He was very loving and sensitive. John referred to himself as "the disciple whom Jesus loved."

Jesus committed the keeping of His mother to John. This placed him in a position where he could interpret the life of Jesus better, perhaps, than any of the Gospel writers. The more you know about the personality and circumstances of the writer, the better equipped you become to understand his purpose in writing his discourse. Also, the book becomes more interesting when you have some acquaintance with the author.

Themes for expository sermons from the Book of John -- Chapters 1-10.

"Christ's power in the Christian"	John 1:18
"Is seeing believing?"	John 2:23, 24
"The love of God"	John 3:14-16
"Witnessing of the truth"	John 3:32-36
"A sermon by the well-side"	John 4:7-26
"Four reasons for believing in Jesus"	John 5:30-47
"The loaves and fishes"	John 6:1-14.
"The final authority in religion"	John 6:66-69
"What the world said about Jesus"	John 7:1-36
"What Jesus said about Himself"	John 8:12-30
"A cure for blindness"	John 8:1-14

Themes for expository sermons from the Lord's Prayer.

When you pray, say, "Our Father, which art in Heaven..."

>We are to talk to the Father directly, not recite prayers.
>Jesus came to reveal God as the Father.
>What is God like?
>What is His purpose in the earth?

"Hallowed by thy name."

>How do we magnify the Lord?
>How do we praise and exalt His name?
>What are some of the names of God?
>For every basic human need and conflict, there is a corresponding name of God.
>How do we go in His name?

"Thy kingdom come, thy will be done on earth as it is in heaven."

> A kingdom means "king's domain."
> How is the kingdom of God distinct from the kingdom of darkness?
> We are living in the "kingdom" when we are in obedience to His authority. In a kingdom, everything is owned by the king. The people are stewards of the king's property. Christians recognize God's ownership. Adam and Eve lived in perfect peace and joy when God owned everything. When they took possession of life, they lost dominion.

"Give us this day our daily bread."

> God wants us to look to Him as our source in life.
> God does not exist to solve our problems. Problems exist to motivate us to pray. The best way to live is to live with the realization that we need God every day.

"Forgive us our debts, as we forgive us our debtors."

> Jesus taught that God will not forgive us if we refuse to forgive one another. To forgive means to let go; to disassociate from the offense. If we don't forgive, we become bitter, and we become bound.

"And lead us not into temptation, but deliver us from evil."

> God never tempts us, but He does have us in a world of darkness so we will have choices in life. His will for us is good.
> To deliver us from evil does not mean, "God, don't let anything bad happen to me." Rather, it means, "God, help me to stay pure in a defiled world. Help me not to become influenced by the "kosmos" around me. Help me to guard my heart from bitterness when people let me down in life."

To Summarize

Diligently and prayerfully read the Bible to get the point, purpose and significance of its statements. Again, the function of a man of God is not to use the Bible to communicate his social commentary, but to be used by God to communicate a message of hope, life, and righteousness to people who need desperately to hear from God.

The discovery of the best in the Scriptures will ultimately, of course, depend upon the man. What we see in the text depends upon what we are. A **sincere, consecrated, educated man** will tend to see what is overlooked or unseen by those not possessing these qualities.

He will be further aided in his selection of themes if he keeps in touch with the needs of the people he leads. A man who loves God and loves people will readily recognize in the Scriptures those truths that have significance for the lives of the people he seeks to help, as he seeks to unfold to them the truths of divine revelation.

John Newton
Slave trading ship captain, and later an English pastor, and composer of the hymn "Amazing Grace"

The Introduction

The three steps of progress:
- ☐ Explanation
- ☐ Introduction
- ☐ Proposition

Explanation

Explain the background of the passage to be treated. Give the connection of the Scripture passage to its context. This may mean one or two verses, a paragraph, a chapter, or another logical division. This will give the congregation a roaming view of the content of the Scripture, and may help create interest in Bible knowledge.

The next step is to arouse an interest in the topic to be discussed. This is done by showing the relationship which the Scripture has to modern life. It is usually not difficult to find some situation in current events to illustrate the principle in the Bible. Technology has changed, but people and their basic personal and relational problems are still the same. Actually, God has not changed either.

WARNING: Merely explaining the Bible will not make it interesting. One must succeed in showing that the theme is a vital and current one, and that the principle involved can be applied to the listener's lives.

Proposition

Let the people know in the beginning the basic thought you want to develop. Make it clear as to where you are going. Then you develop the scriptural ideas, and conclude by reminding them about what you have just said.

Spark their interest.

Find the point which will be interesting and helpful to the congregation. How will you know what is interesting? You can only know that by knowing your people. The more faithful you are in personal ministry, sharing with the people their joys and sorrows, hopes and fears, the more you will know their interests and be able to find the particular phase of each topic that will be attractive to them.

Focus on a theme that is helpful to your people.

It may be interesting to know how many miles it is from Jerusalem to Jericho, or how far it is across the Sea of Galilee, but the important thing is how far the sermon will take them in their own walk of faith.

Examples from Mark:
- "He found nothing but leaves"   Mark 11:1-25
- "This poor widow cast in more"   Mark 11:27 - 12:44
- "Watch"   Mark 13:37
- "Large upper room furnished"   Mark 14:1-26;   see 14:15

- "I will go before you into Galilee"   Mark 14:27-52; see 14:28

Purpose of the Introduction

The first part of the introduction is simply to relate the theme to the book as a whole. The preacher must use all his powers to interest his hearers in a discussion of the theme. The purpose is to attract attention, and to create an atmosphere of positive anticipation and interest in the discussion.

Illustration: John 1:16.
"And of his fullness have all we received, and grace for grace."

We might say to the audience, "did you ever stop to think that in the new birth something of His personality becomes a part of us?" With this statement, we should get their attention. But then we might further ask, "what is the fullness referred to in the text?" This should stimulate even more interest. Then we might say, "and here is the proposition -- the third step. I propose to show you from this first chapter what this fullness is, in what sense we receive it, and in what measure it flows into our lives".

Steps in the Main Division of a Sermon

Well-organized sermons should classify, group, and arrange the main points so that it flows in a logical and sequential pattern. When a message is clearly and effectively divided, the audience will be more able to recall both the material used and also the development of the discourse. They will be able to "get the point" when the supporting points are constructed and presented with skill.

Illustration:

Luke 12:13-30 (This is the familiar story of the rich man who said, "I will tear down my barns and build bigger barns to store my wealth. I have it made." God replied, "You fool. Your time is up. Tonight is it."[74])

---

[74] Paraphrase, Ernest Weaver

Four divisions of the lesson:

☐ His **Fortune**	Luke 12:16-17	*"The ground of a certain rich man brought forth plentifully."*
☐ His **Folly**	vs. 18-19	*"Soul, take thine ease, eat, drink, and be merry."*
☐ His **Fate**	vs. 20	*"Thou fool. This night thy soul shall be required of thee..."*
☐ **Foolish Followers**	vs. 21	*"So is he that layeth up treasure for himself, and is not rich toward God."*

The Purpose of Making Divisions

Clear sermon divisions make it easy for the hearers to remember what was said. This is particularly true if they are constructed in a logical sequence, and in a cohesive style, such as alliteration (beginning each phrase with a word beginning with the same letter of the alphabet. (Note the previous example.)

Analogy

A sermon based on an analogy is one of the best types of sermons, because it can stimulate the imagination of the listener, and is a natural form of illustration. It has been determined in studies that the ability to think in analogies is one of the most accurate gages of human intelligence.

Jesus Christ was the master of analogies. When he taught people who lived by the sea, He said, "You shall be fishers of men." When He spoke to farmers, He taught them the ways of God by speaking of people as plants, or their minds as the soil in which the seeds of the Word are planted. He made sheep analogous of Christians, and described wicked people with metaphors of goats, swine, serpents, wolves, etc. He took objects or concepts familiar to the people and used similarities to illustrate spiritual truths.

Example

"**The parable of the Sower**"   (Matthew 13, Mark 4)
Note: When the disciples asked Jesus why he taught the multitude in parables, He did not reply, "to make it simple and clear." Jesus said,

> *"Unto you it is given to know the mystery of the kingdom of God: but unto them that are without, all these things are done in parables: That seeing they may see, and not perceive; and hearing they may hear, and not understand; lest at any time they should be converted, and their sins should be forgiven them."*
> Mark 4:11-12

After Jesus gave the parables, He would then, in a closed session, give the explanation of the analogies to His covenant disciples. The reason: Jesus did not want people to follow Him because they realized the personal profitability. He wanted people who would make a personal covenant with God out of faith and and love.

Having said that, we still profit from looking at God's kingdom in analogies, as long as we are given the correlations.

Sermon divisions:

- The **sower**   The Holy Spirit is the initial and supreme sower of the Word. As vocal believers, or as preachers, we are secondary sowers.

- The **seed**   The sower sows the Word of God, which speaks to the spirit, not just to the mind of man.

- The **soil**   Jesus mentioned four kinds of soil:

    Wayside.   People who are not quite on track. They are religious, but have not been born again, because they haven't repented of their sins. Satan and his demons are like scavenger birds which quickly devour the

	word with secularism, entertainment, earthly wisdom, etc.
Stony ground.	Some people have no spiritual depth. They want to go to heaven, but haven't really repented. They have religion, but not faith in God.
Thorny ground.	These are religious people who are carnal. They are more focused on earthly pursuits than eternal values. They are not living for Jesus; they are living for themselves.
Good ground.	These are people who have been gloriously born again. They have repented of their sins, and have put their full faith in the Lord Jesus Christ. They have a covenant with God, and love Him more than life itself. They have eternal life in their spirit, and they manifest that by the fact that they love the Word, they live life with joy and moral victory, and they love to talk about Jesus and win souls.

Event

The Bible is rich with historical events in the lives of significant people, both great and small, wise and foolish. The world's entertainment is notorious for portraying life without meaning, and sin without consequences. But the scriptures constantly relate human events to the broader perspective of spiritual truth, and therefore make an excellent basis for teaching people truth and wisdom.

Illustration:

Consider a message about the crucifixion of our Lord Jesus Christ from Matthew 27:11-31. The expositor might use for his main divisions:

- The Prisoner.
- The Accusers.
- The Judge.
- The Verdict.

Illustration:

Genesis 3:9: *"Adam, where art thou?".*
Divisions
- This question was addressed to a man after he had sinned.
- It was addressed to a man who, after he had sinned, was trying to hide from God.
- It was addressed to a man after he had sinned for the purpose of restoring him to fellowship.

When to Make your Divisions

The expositor should always study the material to be used before making divisions. The purpose of making divisions is to establish the progression of thought and to define the primary and secondary ideas. Again, the honest preacher is not using scripture to reinforce his own agenda. He is seeking to honestly communicate the wisdom of the Holy Spirit as communicated through the Word of God.

Three Basic Methods of Making Sermon Divisions:

Group

The simplest type of divisions for expository sermons is that which groups together a number of successive verses, and then brings them together under one head.

Illustration: I Corinthians 13
- Verses 1 - 3   Love contrasted.
- Verses 4 - 6   Love analyzed.
- Verses 7-13   Love defended as the supreme gift.

Classify

Another method of producing expository outlines is to read over the scripture and discover, if possible, related ideas under which the material can be classified.

Illustration: "The conversion of Lydia", using Acts 16:13-15 as a basis. This study could be represented under three headings:

1. What Paul did.
2. What Lydia did.
3. What the Lord did.

Arrange

The third method is that of taking a text or verse of Scripture and giving an exposition of the separate words or phrases. This is strictly expository planning.

Illustration:
- The great lake: God's love   *"God so loved the world..."*
- The river: *"...that He gave His only begotten Son...*
- The pitcher: *...That whosoever believeth in him...*
- The draught: *"...(drink) ...everlasting life.*

Having now selected the theme and decided upon the proposition, your next step is to read and reread the portion of Scripture selected. This should be done day by day, at separate intervals, so that there is time for the assimilation of the thought. You will always gain more insights by reading the passage in different sittings, and perhaps in different settings. Take time to meditate on the word, and let it speak to your spirit. Sleep on it, and then read it again. Also, read it in several translations to gain further insights.

Basic Guidelines for Sermon Structure

Be Simple.

As in the love chapter, I Corinthians 13:
1. Love contrasted.
2. Love analyzed.
3. Love defended.

Be Progressive.

As in the illustration given from Genesis 3:9, "Adam, where art thou?"

Be Comprehensive.

Divisions should complete the proposition, as in the illustration from the story of Lydia. This is a study about conversion. When the participation of the preacher, the convert and the Lord are all included, there is nothing more to say about conversion. However, if any of the participants were to be omitted, the scene would be incomplete, and the message would be weakened.

Making a Sermon Interesting

If any sermon is to be effective, it must be interesting to the listeners. The preacher makes a message interesting by involving his own personality or life experiences, by the literary style that he uses, and by his intelligence and wit. You can have excellent ideas, but if you are boring, you will not be an effective communicator.

Personalization

One of the most popular masters of the art of preaching was the Canadian pulpiteer, Ern Baxter. He was frequently asked to preach about eagles. He would begin with a few key references in Scripture to eagles, and the obvious analogies. Then he would tell some interesting facts about the way eagles rear their young. But instead of a dry recitation of bits of information, he would slip into the first person, as if he were one of the eaglets.

He would masterfully paint a word picture of young eagles, snuggled safely in their lofty perch, enjoying the luxury of the delicious morsels provided by the great mother eagle. But one day, something terrible happens. Mom begins to tear away at the nest. "Has mom gone crazy? Oh, no! She's shoving me out of the nest! Goodbye, cruel world!"

The people are at the edge of their seats, because they are there in their minds, in the great nest high above the rocky and bleak terrain that is the eagle's home. They are identifying with the eagle, because the speaker has personalized the message. It is an easy transition to the way God brings us to maturity, and the spiritual principles related to soaring as an eagle Christian on wings of prayer and faith.

Analogies

The human mind cannot really grasp spiritual realities, such as eternity, infinity, the Trinity, etc. However, we can relate to similarities. God had Moses oversee the construction of the tabernacle, which is an analogy of the Church and the kingdom of God. In fact, it is a whole series of analogies. The Old Testament order is full of types and shadows of the eternal order of God. First the physical, then the spiritual. Show people mysteries by first taking them to that which is understood.

Humor.

There are few fruitful preachers who do not manifest a sense of humor in their preaching. Often, there is humor simply in bringing out unexpected similarities. A writer for the Wall Street Journal, (April 14, 1995) for example, wrote a brilliant article about the Speaker of the House, Newt Gingrich. Newt was pictured as going to Pharaoh Clinton's palace, saying, "Let my people go." He even had his ten articles in the Contract with America engraved on two stone tablets, and promised serious plagues on the Clinton court if he did not free the people.

Humor can be inserted through voice characterizations or graphic mannerisms. If the speaker has really meditated on the story, and has personalized the message, he should be able to express this in a modern vernacular, or even through local jargon.

Of course, there are times when humor is inappropriate. Pulpit humor should never cause embarrassment to anyone, and should never be profane or suggestive. The best humor is natural, and not just an obvious attempt to get people laughing at the beginning of a discourse.

Visual Illustrations

This can involve using charts or main point outlines on an overhead projected screen, or major props. Aimee Semple McPherson, founder of the Foursquare Gospel Church, was noted for using vivid illustrated sermons, even to the point of driving a motorcycle onto the platform, dressed in a policeman's uniform. Some preachers have set up tents by the pulpit to develop the story of Achan, or the tabernacle.

Dramatization

A skilled preacher who plans ahead can recruit a friend or two to make a fascinating drama a part of the sermon. This can be done with or without costumes, sets, or stage lighting. A good dramatic reading monologue can be effective, but "two are better than one."

Action and Motion

With the advent of cordless microphones, modern preachers have more freedom of movement today, even if they are addressing large audiences. There are times when it is very effective to not only walk around the platform, but to walk down into the aisle. If you are talking about a fall, you might take a fall, if you can do it without personal bodily harm. You might sit in a chair for a few minutes, or even on the floor. The danger is in movement that is not appropriate to what is being said. If you are pacing the platform for no apparent reason, you will appear nervous. This will make the people nervous and less attentive. Any gesture that is overdone or without apparent purpose will be distracting.

Pastor Jim has been reading the biography of Billy Sunday.

Originality

    This is the quality that is characteristic of so many of the great preachers. If people perceive that you are parroting some other preacher, they will quickly lose respect and interest. Billy Sunday was interesting because, as a professional athlete who was saved out of a rough lifestyle, he was extreme in his gestures, given to shouting, leaping, and running. But the people knew that it was his style. They would be disappointed if he tried to be as dignified as other preachers.

    Every successful preacher will have imitators. But the imitators will never have the results of the original. That is because God did not design us to all look or sound alike. It's fine to learn from many different role models, but we must each find our own level, and be imitators of God as dear children, not carbon copies of another speaker.

**Originality is attained in three ways:
intense study, apt illustration,
and appropriate application.**

There is no variation from this rule. It works every time. Any person that possesses these qualities, even when presented in a very ordinary way, will be interesting. Conversely, any sermon which lacks them, even when delivered by a good man of God with average ability, will necessarily be uninteresting.

Intense Study

Study the text in the light of the entire book, in order to find out its purpose and to catch its spirit. The first aim should be to know what the original text meant. The second objective is to understand the text within the logical context of the entire book. You can profit from the study of commentaries and other sermons, but that will not be as valuable as the direct study of the Bible in the context of the Bible. If you read it carefully and thoroughly, you will find that the Bible is its own best commentary, and it interprets its own types.

Apt Illustration

A young man came to Jesus and said, "Master, make my selfish brother divide the inheritance with me!" Instead of the expected response, Jesus immediately began to teach him and the people around him by using a human illustration. *"Take heed, and beware of covetousness,"* replied the Master, *"for a man's life consisteth not in the abundance of the things which he possesseth."* Then He illustrated the point. *"The ground of a certain rich man brought forth plentifully,"* and He went on to tell the story. After He had shown the man's folly in thinking that money could bring fulfillment, He applied the truth of the story. He said, *"So is he that layeth up treasure for himself and is not rich in God."* The illustration served as both explanation and application.

People in general need to have their problems interpreted by the Word of God rather than human wisdom, no matter how much of a genius the speaker may be. The Bible preacher needs to know the Word of God, and he needs to know the people. Every visit with his people will help to reveal their joys and sorrows, hopes and fears, and should help to reveal to the pastor their need of divine help and grace. The ability to see these vital relationships between the needs of the people and the Scriptures will increase as the preacher's knowledge of human nature and his observations increase.

Appropriate Application

A sermon may be profound, accurate, logical, and even funny; but if it doesn't have practical application, it will not be effective. Our goal is to build life-changing sermons, not crowd-building theatrics. If the people leave thinking "it's too bad that Brother George wasn't here," then the preacher has missed it. They need to have a sense that they have heard from God for their own situation. They need to go out different from the way they were coming in. They need to be challenged, inspired, and motivated to be more like Jesus in deed as well as in words.

The Sermon's Conclusion

The basic purpose of the conclusion is to apply the proposition of the message to the lives of the people. You cannot devote too much forethought to this part of the sermon. If you fail here, the sermon fails. If you succeed, a very ordinary sermon can become effective. Sometimes a very fine discourse fails because the final five minutes leave the people dangling, or aimless.

The conclusion may also be rendered ineffective by being too abrupt. The speaker is unable to clearly and concisely define the purpose and direction of his discourse. He feels rushed for time because he has lost the attention of the people. Old expressions are floating around in his mind, such as "if you haven't struck oil in forty minutes, stop boring." As a family near the back is gathering up their coats and heading for the door, he blurts out as desperate, "and in conclusion." But he tries to squeeze in the last point and let it suffice for a climax, and it falls flat. He failed to allow enough time for an appropriate conclusion, and he does not leave the people with a sense of purpose or conviction about anything. "Mighty Casey has struck out."

Basic Principles in the Preparation of a Conclusion

- Know exactly the central point of your message, and keep it in mind throughout your discourse. Any farmer knows that the way to plow a straight furrow is to fix your eye on a distant object. If you focus on the area just ahead of the tractor, you will look back and see a crooked line. You must keep your eye on the goal, or you will wind up "chasing rabbits." (This is a preacher's expression meaning "getting off the subject and talking about whatever comes into your head.)

- Know the steps by which you expect to accomplish this purpose. A conclusion may include a brief repetition of the main points of the lesson. At least, the ideas should be communicated and reinforced. Then their relationship to the central theme should be clarified and reiterated.

- Have enough sense to quit when you have delivered the key message, even if you can think of more things to say. In other words, quit when you're through. If you get a reputation for preaching "the everlasting gospel," people will get in the habit of tuning you out, or even of staying home.

- The danger of an unprepared or ill-prepared conclusion is, that the preacher is likely to be soaring around, in an almost hopeless plight, looking for a place to land. Not finding one, he keeps on soaring, and usually has to surrender after tiring his audience. You may see yourself as soaring like an eagle in the heights of the spirit, but the people may be thinking about buzzards.

Basic Methods of Concluding a Sermon

Recapitulation

Restate the main headings to make more decisive your arguments, or to make the proposition clear and concise. If a speaker has good divisions to his sermon, he will strongly reinforce them, as well as the basic topic. The people will tend to appreciate the sense or order and thought that went into the message.

CAUTION: If the message is highly emotional, do not use recapitulation as a conclusion. The emotional sermon calls for a quick and decisive response. You do not just want people to think something, you want them to feel and act a certain way. Generally, if you are primarily a teacher, you will have a clearly defined outline, and should recapitulate in the conclusion. If the nature of the message is more inspirational than informational, then you will be wise to conclude with something more emotional.

A Good Illustration

This can be especially effective if the illustration is personal and directly relevant to the message. Don't make up a story or relate something that happened to someone else and claim it as your own experience, because honesty is part of Christianity. Of course, there are also excellent illustrations of any principle from history, if you are willing to dig them out in study.

An Appeal

If you make an appeal, it must be directly related to the message. There are times when you want to make an appeal for those who want to be born again. If so, then you should preach on repentance and faith, and genuinely lead people to Jesus. Today we are so intent on filling an altar that we make it easy for people to make a half-hearted commitment to an ambiguous goal. The Bible does not say that we are to "accept Jesus Christ." It says to repent, and to be born again. Don't say, "Do you want to go to heaven?" Everyone wants to go to heaven, but that doesn't save them. Many people want to go to heaven when they die, but don't want to stop sinning or serve Jesus.

When Charles Finney preached during the Great Awakening in New England, he would preach with great fervor and spiritual power. He would then invite people to a "mourner's bench", where they would often weep over their sins. Sometimes, he would say, "If you really want to repent and get right with God, come back tomorrow and I'll tell you how to be born again." It is said that of the thousands of people who were converted through his ministry, ninety-five percent of the converts joined a local church and became solid Christians. Compare that to our results today.

Charles Finney
1792-1875

On occasion, the message from God may indeed by about financial giving. It may be appropriate to end a message with an appeal for an offering. Just make sure that God is telling you to do so. If you get a reputation for frequently appealing for money, the people may get the idea that "he does not really love us. He just wants our money." Some pastors have lost many families who quit the church, and they almost never tell him the real reason.

There are other appeals that can be given at the end of a good sermon. Keep in mind that most of the time we are preaching to Christians. We are called to feed the sheep. Therefore, most of the teaching and preaching should be directed at believers. There are times to encourage the people to pray for one another, or to plan a time of hospitality. An appeal may be given to make expressions of love or forgiveness, or to commit to someone for personal accountability. Other applications should be obvious.

Worship

If your message is about praise and worship, then it should create a thirst in the people for the presence of God. There could be no better conclusion than to lead them in at least a few appropriate songs, especially ones that reinforce the preceding message of the sermon.

A Song

All "special music" should flow with the service, and not become a showcase for someone's talent. Just because you have a soprano who can almost hit the notes and sing along with a Sandy Patti soundtrack does not mean that the song will minister. Having said that, it can be very effective to have the "special song" at the end of the message. This will work only if the song is directly echoing the thought of the sermon, and if the singer or group is skilled and anointed.

A Well Chosen Quotation

This is generally for the devotional or inspirational type of sermon. This could be a quotation from the Scriptures, from another preacher, or from one of the poets. (It's always good to quote from Shakespeare or some famous literary figure. This makes you look well read.) A good quotation from a famous hymn can also be very effective.

The character of the conclusion is not determined by the type of sermon, whether expository, topical, or inferential, but is rather decided by the didactic or hortatory (emotional, devotional) elements by which it closes. Do that which is appropriate to the moment.

Avoid becoming too predictable. Use a variety of methods for best results.

The purpose for all preaching is:
To persuade.
To bring conviction.
To lead to action.

Chapter 10

Bible Study Methods

Effective preaching is the result of diligent Bible study.

Introduction

> *"The fruits of Bible Study are largely determined by how the Bible is studied."*
> Irving L. Jensen

Although there are numerous methods of Bible study, there are just two basic approaches to Bible study which greatly affect the way the preacher handles truth in the pulpit. One approach is called "inductive"; the other, "deductive". While statistical support for the following statement is not available, it is a safe generalization that too many ministers utilize the deductive approach at the expense of the inductive. The reason may be force of habit, ignorance as to what they are doing, or lack of careful evaluation of personal Bible study habits and the fruits of their methods of Bible study.

The Deductive Approach.

Begin with a concept, then search the scriptures.

The scholar employing this method begins with a general principle, concept or conclusion. He then searches for scripture to ascertain whether the conclusion is true. Many use this approach to find proof texts for their private interpretations, or to force scripture to say what they want it to say. This preacher has a tendency to look for scriptures to reinforce or support his previously determined opinions and interpretations. There is a danger in this approach of communicating to scripture rather than scripture communicating to you.

The Inductive Approach.

> Begin with the Word of God, and then develop the concept.

The deductive approach, by contrast, can be said to be more "subjective" in its general use. That is, the thoughts and personality of the researcher greatly influence the conclusions being developed, as opposed to being "objective," where he is looking only at the facts presented.

For example, many preachers have studied the subject of divorce and remarriage on behalf of a divorced family member who wants to remarry. Some have even looked into the subject while in that situation themselves. Often, they will look for an interpretation that will encourage, or at least excuse the action they really want to take. The person who is not personally in that frustrating position has the capacity to be more "objective," because he has no vested interest in the verdict.

Obviously, we are all influenced by our preconceived ideas, whether we admit it or not. We have a difficult time being entirely objective in interpreting the scripture, and that is why we need to listen to other pastors and teachers, and to be very sensitive to the Holy Spirit.

Characteristics of the Inductive Method.

It is **analytical** in its methodology.

> Merrill C. Tenny said, "In order to ascertain exactly what a body of text says, one should employ the analytical method." [75] Analysis involves observation for structure. This means that we look objectively at the way the scripture is put together. We make honest observations of the parts of the passage under study and the relationship of the parts to the whole.

---

[75] Merrill C. Tenny, "The Genius of the Gospel" pg 135

It is **scientific** in its order of procedure.

>The first step is observation: What do you see?
>Interpretation follows: What does it mean?
>Application is demanded: How does this relate to me?

Procedure for Inductive Study.

This kind of study must involve a thorough reading and rereading of the text studied. There are basic and obvious things to look for in evaluating any communication. What does it say? Who said what? What is the main idea? When did it take place? Where? Why? How?

Observe the main trend of thought.

Most Biblical writers do not announce the purpose of their writings. It is the student's task to discover the central theme of the text. He should always seek to distinguish between the primary and the subordinate ideas. Many people generally lack the ability to see the outline in the text of a discourse. Perhaps it is like the ability to discern the skeletal structure of another person by observing his features and gait. This takes practice and effort.

Observe the unexpected or unnoticed. There are multitudes of fascinating and profitable thoughts that can be gleaned by repetitive rereading of Bible passages. You can read a verse a hundred times, and then some fresh truth will jump out at you the hundred and first time you read it. No wonder the writer to the Hebrews said that the Bible was "alive and powerful." [76]

Recognize the laws of composition.

Construct a title for the passage under study that states the central thought or theme that the author wants to communicate. Then look for several key phrases or words that will encapsulate the sections which support the central idea. Discern between the basic ideas and the supporting illustrations, allegories, or examples added.

---

[76] Hebrews 4:12

Observe the major divisions and write titles for them.

Often the overall purpose of a book can be seen by observing the main intent of each large division within that book. The major divisions are the primary concepts the writer has to communicate regarding the theme of the passage. They are the development of his theme.

Observe the paragraphs within each major division. Give each paragraph a title. Each paragraph has a unifying thought which develops the main divisions or explains the major divisions of the book.

Interpret – "What does it Mean?"

A prerequisite for correct interpretation is correct observation. Correct interpretations are not hastily developed. It is here that basic rules of hermeneutics are employed.

Everything essential to salvation and Christian living is clearly revealed in scripture. The Bible is God's truth and revelation to man. Unlike the Mormons, we have an accurate text in the canon of scripture. The Bible is amazingly cohesive, despite the authorship of over forty writers over a span of sixteen hundred years. The Bible is historically accurate, and has been verified by many different sources.

Interpret every word literally unless this leads to contradiction or absurdity. If you cannot interpret a passage literally, you should have a valid reason for seeing it as figurative, or prophetic. Many wrong doctrines have come out of interpreting figurative language as literal, such as the Mormon idea of a human, physical God coming from the many anthropomorphisms in scripture.

Determine the truth intended by the original author through that figure of speech -- no more and no less. Avoid the temptation to make a Bible writer say more than he has said. Interpret the text both in light of immediate content and greater context.

How is the Message to be Applied?

The student of scripture should not be concerned with what he does to scripture, but with what scripture does to him. The Kingdom of God is a counter-culture compared to our people-oriented societies. This is clearly illustrated in the Sermon on the Mount, where Jesus startled the multitude with a radically different view of life. His view of the world centered in God, love, and a values system based on that which was spiritual and eternal. Our values tend to be focused on the temporal and physical world.

In preaching, we are constantly faced with the need to challenge people to focus their thinking toward a Christian worldview: that is, a view of life that centers on Jesus, rather than on the individual. Also, a Christian worldview of life leads us to repentance, faith, and obedience to God, as well as to functional altruism in our lifestyle. Our goal is not only to get people to think correctly, but also to live accordingly. For example, the popular notion that the definition of grace is "unmerited favor" tends to lead people to the conclusion that "since my lifestyle has nothing to do with my salvation, I can sin and get away with it." A careful study of the Greek word *"charis"* will reveal that it is much more than a freebie. Grace has to do with that which God supernaturally imparts to us to enable us to live righteously and to bless others.

If grace were simply unmerited favor, then the message of grace would teach us that we are just all sinners who cannot live a holy life anyway. However, notice what the Apostle Paul said of the effect of the teaching of Biblical grace.

> *"For the grace of God that bringeth salvation hath*
> *appeared to all men,*
> *Teaching us that, denying ungodliness and worldly lusts,*
> *we should live soberly, righteously, and godly, in*
> *this present world;*
> *Looking for that blessed hope, and the glorious*
> *appearing of the great God and our Saviour Jesus*
> *Christ;*

> *Who gave himself for us, that he might redeem us from all iniquity, and purify unto himself a peculiar people, zealous of good works.* [77]

Communication

We really communicate the truth of the gospel initially by the way we live, and by the ways we respond to other people. Jesus gained an audience because He demonstrated a pure heart of love and compassion, and then showed that He had the supernatural power to do something for them. With that as His basis, He was then able to tell them about the radically different reality of the things of the Spirit.

We also communicate through the "foolishness of preaching." God chose to use anointed people as the primary messengers of His truth, rather than angels. As fallible human vessels, we are often preaching to ourselves as well as to our audience, but we should at least be on the right track when we preach.

We communicate truth both by teaching and preaching. Sometimes it's difficult to distinguish the two, especially since most of us do both, and usually in the same discourse.

Preaching	Teaching
Emphasis on the inspirational.	Emphasis on informational.
Followed by signs and wonders.	More notes than signs, less wondering.
Focus on "Rhema" word.	Verify everything with the "Logos".
More persuasive.	More structured.
For some, an excuse for a lack of preparation.	For others, an excuse for a lack of anointing.

The overlap potential is obvious. Some preachers are very well organized, and communicate plenty of practical information. Some teachers are very inspirational or dramatic. Generally, such overlap is good. All preachers should leave people with a greater understanding

---

[77] Titus 2:11-14

of aspects of God and the Christian life, and teachers should be inspiring.

A distinguishing mark of the Christian preacher is that his is not just communicating the words of Jesus. He is communicating Jesus. We are the "ministers of Christ." [78] We do not just have His ideas in our minds. We have His Spirit in our hearts. We have to power to do what He did. He lives in us. The people want to see Jesus in us, and not just His creeds.

All false religions are based on the sayings of a human teacher, master, or "guru." Millions of people base their lifestyles and eternal hopes on the writings of Mary Baker Eddy, or Confucius, or Buddha, or Mohammed. But we are not merely parroting the wise sayings of our leader. We are walking in daily communion with Him, and are empowered by Him to do more than merely speak words about Him. We literally bring people to Him. **Jesus does not just inform, He transforms.**

The Value of an Inductive Chart

An inductive chart records and represents the student's observations and interpretations. When used as a visual aid, it fosters retention of content. [79] As the Bible says in Hezekiah 14:12, "one picture is worth a thousand words" [80] Of course, this is a broad generalization. Some pictures are lousy, and worth only a few words. The less said about them, the better. On the other hand, a really brilliant paragraph can illustrate some things better than pictures.

An inductive chart helps us see the whole pattern of thought simultaneously. This makes it easy to recall, because it forms a mental picture of the material in the mind. It also helps to integrate the various parts of the material, so that the whole pattern is quickly and accurately communicated. It helps us to identify and articulate the key thought in each division, and facilitates the development of each division by its paragraphs. A good chart helps to also see the various progressions, contrasts, comparisons, topics, and word studies involved in the discourse.

---

[78] I Corinthians 4:1
[79] Translation: "it helps you remember more."
[80] Reversed Standard Edition

This chart helps us to distinguish the primary ideas from the supportive or subordinate points related to them. It also enables the teacher to organize his thoughts more concisely. You could say that a chart visually defined areas of study, and makes the structure of the material more easily discerned.

Tools Necessary for Inductive Study

The Holy Spirit's Guidance

The first and most important asset is an honest and humble dependence on the Holy Spirit. He is the divine teacher. The truths of God are reasonable, but they are not birthed in human reason. Indeed, or rationalizations and carnal musings will always lead us to wrong conclusions, because we tend to focus on the material and temporal world. Wisdom is seeing things from God's point of view, because He sees the whole picture from the perspective of the spiritual as well as the natural; from the standpoint of eternity and infinity. Human reason, in and of itself, will always result in error and confusion.

An Unmarked Study Bible

A major part of any concentrated study should be done in one version of the Bible. Your study Bible should have a paragraph arrangement of verses. This helps to confirm the writer's organization of thoughts. The American Standard Version (1991) is a very accurate translation from the original languages, and a study edition is available with that translation.

A Binder and Paper

We recommend the standard $8\frac{1}{2}$" x 11" paper (U.S., or standard-sized paper for your locality), both for cost and for convenience. You can get a good amount of material on a page and still be fairly portable. The loose-leaf binder is best, because you can reorganize pages as you progress.

Writing Instruments

You should also have colored pencils or felt pens so that you can color code your notes. Of course, it is a good idea to later type your notes, or to enter them into a computer. This is idea, because it is so easy to make changes, corrections, and highlights.

Relation to Expository Preaching

A good inductive chart becomes the outline for an expository sermon. An expository sermon is an effort to explain, illustrate and apply scripture to life. It tends to follow the sequence of ideas as expressed by the original writer, with amplification, explanation, and practical application. This correlates perfectly with the inductive approach to Bible study.

We cannot over emphasize the importance of a sound inductive method for the work of an expositor. No matter what other qualifications a preacher of the Bible may have -- spiritual, technical, educational or cultural -- if he is deficient in his logical approach to the scripture he will be seriously crippled as a reliable interpreter of the sacred scriptures.

A competent expounder of divine truth must rigidly discipline himself to study every theme of scripture in a thoroughly inductive fashion. Only by complete induction, in which all the particular facts or cases in question are exhaustively considered, can scripturally dependable thematic generalizations be made.

The relevance of such logical handling of the Word of God becomes apparent when the task of the expositor is defined. His job, it must be remembered, is not to expound on the musings of science, philosophy, or religion; nor on what saith men's creeds and criticisms. His mission is clear and inescapable. What saith the Word of God? That is the question of vital import to him.

This being the case, he must study every theme of the Bible inductively: collating, observing, analyzing, and classifying all of the passages pertinent to the subject being treated. This is the only valid procedure to take in order to find out what God has revealed on any particular subject. [81]

---

[81] Merril F. Unger, Principles of Expository Preaching pg. 100

I just hate it when he does that.
He thinks he's so-o-o spiritual.

Basic Goals of a Good Sermon

- ♦ Begin with a deeply felt truth.
- ♦ Justify it from scripture.
- ♦ Explain it in modern terms.
- ♦ Illuminate it with illustration.
- ♦ Make it memorable.
- ♦ Apply it to a current scene or need.
- ♦ Persuade a suitable response.

Ways to Achieve those Goals

Apply the text to: Yourself, to your neighbors, and to God.

Example: The Fruit of the Spirit. [82]

- ☐ When the Holy Spirit is working in my life, He will cause me to love others more than I love myself. He will give me an abiding sense of joy and peace, regardless of the circumstances...

- ☐ The abiding presence of the Holy Spirit in my neighbor's life as well as my own will result in a mutual caring and friendship, communication, honesty, patience with one another,...

- ☐ The Holy Spirit will teach me about the things of God. He will motivate me to pursue a deeper relationship with Him, always glorify the Son, and will enable me to pray in perfect harmony with the will of the Father...

Apply the text to: The World, the Church, the Individual.

Example: The Return of Christ.

Ask the questions: who, what, why, when, where, how?

Example: *"Arise and be baptized, washing away your sins!"* From Acts 22:16

Who is making the statement?	Anaias
Who is to be baptized?	Saul of Tarsus
What is the objective?	Water baptism.
Why?	The remission of sins.
When?	After his conversion.
Where?	A large body of water on the way.
How?	Immersion in water.

---

[82] Galatians 5:22-23

Develop comparisons: from something to something.

Examples: *"To turn them from darkness to light"*
"He has turned my mourning into dancing for me."

Think of various ways to apply that statement, such as:

- From sickness to health.
- From defeat to victory.
- From despair to hope.

Arrange the text in a uniform pattern.

Example: **The Shepherd Psalm.**

A. My Shepherd gives me:
   1. Provision   (1-2)
   2. Propitiation   (3)
   3. Protection   (4-5)
   4. Promotion   (6)

B. I shall not lack (want):
   1. Pasture.
   2. Peace.
   3. Pathway.
   4. Protection.
   5. Preparation.
   6. Promise.

C. The Shepherd daily:
   1. Feeds the sheep.
   2. Guides the sheep.

  3. Comforts the sheep.
  4. Brings the sheep safely home.

 D. A Table of:
  1. Plenty in the Presence of Poverty (1-2).
  2. Salvation in the Presence of Sin (3).
  3. Life in the Presence of Death (4-5).
  4. Eternity in the Presence of Time (6).

Apply the text to various areas.

Example: *"From glory to glory:"*

- From the glory of the law to the glory of the Gospel.
- From the glory of the new birth to the glory of full stature.
- From the glory of a servant to the glory of a son.
- From the glory of the church to the glory of the kingdom.

Example: *"That in all things Christ might have preeminence:"* over:

- The world.
- The church.
- The family.
- Me.

Develop the meaning of a word or idea.

Example: Hebrews 7:25; the word "uttermost" is applicable to:
time, position, or character; thus:

- An Undying Salvation.
- An Unchanging Salvation.
- A Universal Salvation.

"The four Kinds of Love:"

Greek word   Definition

- ☐ *eros*   physical attraction
- ☐ *phileo*   brotherly love, friendship
- ☐ *storge*   family love
- ☐ *agape*   Godly love, covenant giving of self.

"The Four Kinds of Faith:"

- ☐ Providential.
- ☐ Saving.
- ☐ Particular.
- ☐ Gifted.

In Matthew 5:48, the word "perfect" has the idea of "not yet complete, but advancing toward the goal;" thus,

We are advancing toward:

- ☐ Maturity in God.
- ☐ Fellowship with God.
- ☐ The purpose of God
- ☐ Surrender to God.

I John 1:3-4, "Fellowship"

- ☐ What is this fellowship?
- ☐ What is its basis?
- ☐ What are its limits?
- ☐ What are its benefits?

(Those questions can all be answered from the text).

"Fellowship" = *koinonia* = friendship, partnership, sharing, communion.

Other Word Studies

Check the dictionary definitions of such words as "peace, meekness, grace, blessing, virtue, holiness; etc."; also use your thesaurus and theological dictionary.

SOME SUGGESTED TOOLS FOR BIBLE RESEARCH

Bible

King James Version
New International Version
New King James Version Translation

Living Bible
Amplified Bible
Wuest Expanded

Concordance

New Englishman's Greek Concordance (Zondervan)
Englishmanís Hebrew & Chaldee Concordance (Zondervan)
Greek-English Concordance to the New Testament, J. B. Smith (Herald Press)
Strong's Exhaustive Concordance (Abingdon)
Young's Analytical Concordance (Eerdman's)

Lexicon

Analytical Greek Lexicon (Zondervan)
Analytical Hebrew & Chaldee Lexicon, B. Davidson (Mac Donald)
Greek-English Lexicon, Arndt & Gingrich (University of Chicago Press)
Greek-English Lexicon, T. S. Green (Zondervan)
Hebrew-English Lexicon, W. Gesenius (Oxford)
New Thayer's Greek-English Lexicon (Evangel)

Lexical Aid

Dictionary of Old Testament Words, Aaron Pick (Kregel)
Expositor's Greek Testament, W. Robertson Nicoll (Eerdman's)
Expository Dictionary of New Testament Words, W. E. Vine (Revell)
Grammatical Insights into the New Testament, N. Turner (T & T Clark)

Lexical Aids for Students of New Testament Greek, B.
    Metzer (Theological Book Agency, Dist.)
New Testament Words, William Barclay (SCM Press)
New Testament Word Studies, J. A. Bengal (Kregel)
Old Testament Word Studies, William Wilon (Kregel)
Synonyms of the New Testament, R. C. Trench
Synonyms of the Old Testament, R. B. Gridlestone
    (Eerdman's)
Syntax of the Moods and Tenses, E. Burton (T & T Clark)
Theological Dictionary of the New Testament, Ed. Kittle
    (Eerdman's)
Word Pictures in the New Testament, A. T. Robertson
    (Broadman Press)
Word Studies in the New Testament, M. R. Vincent
    (Eerdman's)

Bible Geography

All the Animals of the Bible Lands, G. Cunsdale
    (Zondervan)
Animals and Birds of the Bible, B. L. Goddard (A P & A)
Baker's Bible Atlas, Pfeiffer (Baker)
Geography of the Bible, D. Baly (Harper and Brothers)
The Macmillan Bible Atlas (Macmillan)
Oxford Bible Atlas (Oxford Press)
The Wycliffe Historical Geography of Bible Lands, Pheiffer
    and Vos. (Moody)

Historical Background

Archaeology & Bible History, J. P. Free (Van Kampen
    Press)
Archaeology and the Old Testament, Unger (Zondervan)
The Bible and Archeology, J. A. Thomson (Pasternoster
    Press)
Bible History -- Old Testament, A. Edersheim
    (Eerdman's)
Old Testament Bible History, Edersheim (Eerdman's)
The Life and Times of Jesus the Messiah, A. Edersheim
    (Eerdman's)

217

The Words of Flavius Joseph (Kregel)

This list of research tools is only a small sample of what is available in the field. Visiting a Gospel book store or talking to other ministers is a good way of enlarging the minister's library. Many pastors like to visit book stores that deal in used books. Some of the older out-of-print books can be very helpful to the minister looking for good sermon material. It is advisable to use the suggested Bible research tools during regular Bible devotions and making notes of interesting ideas, and not only when looking for material for a sermon.

Please refer to the section in this text that gives suggestions about keeping an idea file for sermons. One of the most frightening experiences that a young or new minister will face is to be called upon to speak for a special occasion and not have some of the good illustrations that he/she may have read in some religious or secular publication.

Keeping a Homiletics File

Methods and Materials

There are many different ways that the student of the Bible can go about keeping a file of ideas. Some people prefer using an accordion pleat folder with sections labeled. Others use a part of their regular filing cabinet with divided sections. This writer prefers using 4 x 6 index cards and keeping them in a regular 4 x 6 file box.

The 4 x 6 card can be purchased in various colors which makes it possible to use a different color for various subjects. The color red can be used for Salvation (red for the Blood of Christ?). Blue is an excellent color for water baptism, etc. It is best for each individual student to develop a system that will be most meaningful to him/her.

TOPIC SALVATION	SCRIPTURE TEXT	OTHER TEXTS
God's salvation is the result of His love for us.	JOHN 3:16 For God so loved the world…	ROMANS 5:8 But God commandeth His love toward us in that while we were yet sinners…

    Good illustrations or stories can be placed on the reverse side of the card. It is possible that in some cases several cards will be used for a certain topic. In that case the cards should be numbered. It should be noted that there are a number of very fine filing systems on the market for just this purpose.

I want to thank the pulpit committee for designing the new lectern for me.

PRACTICUM

Prepare a five-minute talk, which must contain:

- An introduction.
- Two or three major headings.
- Two or three sub-headings under each major heading.
- Application and Conclusion.

A strict time limit should be enforced.

Rules for the presentation:

You may read the message, speak from written notes, or speak extemporaneously. In any case, you should be animated, maintain eye contact with your audience, and speak with conviction and persuasion.

****

Chapter 11

SERMON OUTLINE METHODS

EFFECTIVE PREACHING: A RESULT OF BIBLE STUDY

Dynamics of Good Outlining

Not too many people remember what they learned about outlining when they were in school, or they just failed pay attention in the first place. Perhaps they were thinking they would never use the information. One of the most useful tools in Bible research and in sermon preparation is the proper use of outlining. Many ministers (and speakers) develop their own system of making notes of their sermon or speech. Keep in mind the fact that you cannot have very useful files if they are not well organized.

The outline is a simple means of developing a plan of presentation. It is not necessary to show all of the details of the topic in the outline, but a good outline will contain the following:

Elements of a Good Outline

1. The order of the parts.
    This order will help the speaker keep from wandering off of the topic and loosing the congregation along the way.

2. The divisions of the subjects.
    A sermon needs to be well organized so that the listeners can see where one idea is completed and another begins.

3. The relationship of the parts.
    A good sermon flows smoothly from one idea to the next, and finally to a logical finish.

    NOTE: Although this is a course in public speaking, rules of good writing generally also apply to good preaching.

Qualities of Good Writing:

Brevity A sermon does not need to be long to be good. The average person can only absorb so much information at any one time.

Clarity A writer must always make sure that the intended audience can clearly understand what is being presented. An acquaintance of this author was so caught up in his own eloquence that if he could not think of a "big" word he would coin or make up one. Someone was overheard to say one day that the church should have dictionaries in the bookracks instead of songbooks.

Cohesion This means that the material in the sermon should flow from one idea to the next in a logical, understandable way. It holds together, and is reasonably identifiable as a unit. One of the hindrances to cohesion is the tendency of some preachers to insert humorous antidotes at the wrong time. Or by telling a story that really does not have any real relevance to the point at hand.

The Form of the Outline

There are several different forms used in outlining. The following is the most traditional.

1. Use Roman numerals (I, II) to indicate the major divisions.
2. Use capital letters (A, B) to indicate the second level.
3. Use Arabic numerals (1. 2) to indicate the third level.
4. Use lower-case letters (a, b) to indicate the fourth level.
5. Use Arabic numerals within parentheses to indicate the fifth level.
6. Use a period after each number or letter.
7. Indent each subdivision approximately five spaces.

    I. The Earth

    A. Sea
    B. Land
       1. Islands
       2. Continents
          a. Northern hemisphere
          b. Southern
II. The Heavens
    A. Physical universe
    B. Supernatural heavens

Types of Sermon Outlines

1. The Character Outline Method

A study of Bible characters is a good tool for imparting wisdom. As we read what God says about Bible men and women, we get a clear picture of what God thinks of them. We thus see responses and attitudes in life which are pleasing or repugnant in the sight of God and are inspired to holy living.

Example

The character of **Moses**

Most of these are found in Exodus, the third and fourth chapters. His characteristics could be arranged under two heads.

              A. His qualifications.
              B. His excuses.

To make the sermon complete we must find the points under two headings. With study we can develop it thus:

A. The qualifications of Moses.
    1. Industry -- Moses kept the flock.
    2. Belief in the supernatural -- "see this great sight".
    3. Veneration -- "Put off thy shoes".
    4. Personal knowledge of God -- "God of thy Father".

B. His excuses.
    1. No reputation -- "Who am I"?
    2. No message -- "What shall I say"?

3. No audience -- "They will not believe".
4. No speaking skills -- "I am not eloquent."
5. No confidence -- "Send whom Thou wilt".

C. Conclusion
1. Follow him to Egypt and notice his message.
2. It did not take much eloquence, but he relied on a demonstration of the power of God.

2. The Key-Word Method.

Sometimes, when reading a portion of Scripture, a certain word or phrase of more or less frequent occurrence is impressed on the mind and suggests a thought around which a sermon can be arranged.

Example:

A. **"Four Looks Toward Sodom"**   Genesis 13:10; 18:16; 19:26; 19:28.

1. Lot's look toward Sodom.
   a. "Lot lifted up his eyes and beheld..."
   b. Lot looked at the natural benefits.

2. The Lord's look
   a. "and the men rose up from thence".
   b. The difference between the world's wisdom and God's wisdom.

3. Lot's wife looked.
   a. Lust of the eye.
   b. "The light of the body is the eye."
   c. "Look not on the wine when it is red..."

4. Abraham's look.
   a. Abraham did not look to the secular world for his fulfillment.
   b. He "looked for a city, whose builder and maker is God."

B. Conclusion
1. Abraham's look typifies the look of the triumphant saint.

2. *"God remembered Abraham and sent Lot out of the midst..."*

Other examples.

- The *"Alls"* in Ephesians 6:18
- The phrase *"kingdom of Heaven"* in Matthew
- *"Under the Sun"* in Ecclesiastes
- The *five "I wills"* of Lucifer in Isaiah 14.
- The five *"I wills"* of Jesus

The Bible is rich in such sermon material.

3. The Pictorial Outline Method.

Sometimes a text brings before the mind a picture from some incident of life, some occupation or like thing. The portraying of this picture and the weaving into it of the spiritual message on the preacher's heart calls forth some of the finest faculties of the mind.

Example: Psalm 16:11   *"Thou wilt show me the path of life..."*

"The Journey of Life"

A. The Guide --"Thou" -- Jesus Christ
   1. His qualifications -- wise, kind, etc.
   2. His experience -- has been over the road.
   3. His interest -- He died for me.

B. The Traveler -- "Me"
   1. Must take the journey.
   2. Have not had experience.
   3. Need just such a guide.

C. The Road -- "Path"
   1. The road is one of many.
   2. It is narrow.
   3. Not many on it.

D. The Destination -- "Life"
   1. Contrast with death.
   2. A delightful anticipation.
   3. A glorious consummation.

This example causes the listener to visualize himself as the "pilgrim" on the path of life, in the same way that John Bunyon wrote the great allegorical "Pilgrim's Progress." The same thought is developed in the old song, "Palms of Victory." Jesus used this kind of allegorical process often in His teaching.

Another example could be: "Teach me to do thy will".

- The teacher -- God.
- The scholar -- "Me."
- The lesson -- "Thy will."

4. The Narrative Outline Method.

The narrative of a Bible event can be very interesting if the preacher has spent adequate time in prayer, and if he knows the details of the account thoroughly. It is helpful here to have a vivid imagination, so that you can deduce from the information given aspects of the characters, as well as the scenes and circumstances related to the event.

Example 1:
Balaam.   (Numbers 22)

Balaam was a prophet. He knew how to pray, and he knew how to hear the voice of God. He was on his way to King Balak's palace. It had not been the best of times for prophets in the land. For one thing, the Israelites seemed to be the only folks around interested in hearing from God, and they were not his clients. An old guy named Moses had a corner on that market. Now Balaam had a client, and it was about time. The rent was past due, and he was so poor he had trouble paying his servants.

He was riding along when his donkey suddenly stopped. He was almost thrown off. He beat the poor animal, and blurted out a few choice words he hadn't learned in Sabbath school. Suddenly, the donkey turned to him and said, "Whoa.... Hey, what it is, man? Haven't I always been a good donkey? Cut me some slack, boss!"

Example 2:
The Road to Damascus   (Acts 9)

Using the same picture of riding a donkey, the preacher might tell of the conversion of Saul of Tarsus on the road to Damascus. Again, rather than dry, factual report, some characterization and animation can be added to communicate the scene in a much more lively fashion. As the preacher describes the future apostle in his self-righteous anger and zeal, he could be bouncing up and down, simulating a rough donkey ride, muttering to himself between clenched teeth about these fanatic heretics in Damascus, and what he was going to do when he got his hands on them....

Example 3:

The Story of Naaman's Healing.   II Kings 5:1-14

A. The remedy needed.
   1. A great man's disease.
   2. The nature of the disease.

B. The remedy advertised (vs. 2-4)
   1. The maid's testimony.
   2. Repeated testimony.

C. The remedy sought (vs. 5-10)
   1. With many.
   2. Among royalty.
   3. His quest rewarded.

D. The remedy equivocated. (verses 11 and 12)
   1. Unfulfilled anticipations.
   2. Unfavorable comparisons.

E. The remedy applied.
   1. He hearkens.
   2. He is humble.
   3. He is healed.

Practical application

The incurable disease, leprosy, is a biblical type of sin. We are all afflicted with this spiritual malady no matter how great we are in the eyes of the world. There is only one remedy for this deadly condition. We must be washed in the blood of Jesus Christ. Just as Naaman had to have a messenger, so we must hear about the cure from one of God's covenant people (Christian). The "advertising" of the gospel is still the method of preaching, and it's not necessarily by the powerful or the brilliant. All God needs is a servant willing to give a message of hope to someone dying.

> *"...it pleased God by the foolishness of preaching to save them that believe."*
> I Corinthians 1:21

The remedy for the terminal disease is not obtained with money, but by repentance and faith. Only when we humble ourselves to obey God's commands will we find the grace we need for salvation. We cannot impress God with our greatness or achievements, but we can impress Him with humility and faith.

Other illustrations of such sermons:

- The man who went down from Jerusalem to Jericho
- Peter and the vision of unclean animals
- Abraham and Isaac
- Joseph in Egypt
- Paul and Silas in jail
- Elijah and Elisha

Our speaker today, Rev. McGilla, is noted for his exceptional ability to appeal for offerings.

5. The Synthetic Outline Method.

In analysis, a single text is composed of a variety of ideas that need to be taken apart and considered separately in order to get the context of the text. In synthesis we take a variety of texts which may be gathered from different books of the Bible and bring them together to get their combined teaching. Each of these methods moves in opposite directions from the other. In analysis we begin with the text and then work out the idea. In synthesis we begin with an idea and gather around it confirmatory and illustrative text.

An idea is essential to the preparing of a sermon outline on the synthetic plan. However, it must be an idea from the Bible itself if it is to be a Biblical sermon.

Example of Synthesis

Consider the illustration of a sermon on Jesus, the Coming One. The preacher may first compile scriptural references relative to the predictions of the second coming of Christ, and then arrange them in a logical order. From this list, he can form the basis of a sermon on eschatology. His list may include the following sub-points:

- He will be seed of woman.
  Genesis 3:15.
- He will be a descendent of Abraham.
  Genesis 22:18
- He will be a descendent of David.
  II Samuel 7:13.
- He will be born in Bethlehem.
  Micah 5:2.
- He will have nails put in hands and feet.
  Psalm 22:16.
- He will not remain in tomb.
  Psalm 16:10.

Now find the verses in the New Testament where these prophecies are fulfilled and put them together to prove God's Word is perfectly fulfilled concerning this "Coming One".

This is but one line of synthetic comparison that is possible regarding Jesus Christ. The histories of Joseph and Moses can be compared point by point with the life of Christ and shown to be the foreshadowing of Jesus. Material objects are often used as analogies or types of Christ, the church, or another reality of the spiritual world. The Temple and its sacrifices may be compared in detail with the person and work of Jesus and shown to be shadows of His work.

(Note: This method is sometimes given as Bible readings.)

6. The Contrast Outline Method

Some texts consist of two contrasted truths setting forth opposite sides of a subject. Such texts are very common, especially in Proverbs, in which some whole chapters consist of groups of contrasts. See, for example: Proverbs 10. Nearly every verse contains a contrastive. Notice the repeated use of the conjunction, "but". Also see Romans 6:23 –

> *"The wages of sin is death;* **but** *the gift of God is eternal life."*

It is self-evident that a text outlined by the contrastive method will have only two main divisions: one for each of the contrasted clauses.

Example: A sermon outline from Romans 6:23:

"Two Pay Days"

A. **Introduction:**
   1. No escape of pay day mentioned here.
   2. Life is spent in service of one of two masters.
   4. We must choose one master or another.

B. **Body:**
   1. *"The Wages of Sin"*
      a. Sin -- the pay master.
      b. Wages -- the pay envelope.
      c. Death -- the payment.

    2. *"The Gift of God is Eternal Life"*.
        a. God -- Paymaster.
        b. Gift -- Pay envelope
        c. Life -- Payment.

C. Conclusion: *"Through Jesus Christ our Lord."*

This reveals the way this gift is bestowed, and how one may leave the service of sin and receive the gift of life. The gift of God is passed down through the hands of a mediator. To ignore the mediator means to miss the gift.

This sermon may be preached in either of two ways. It can be given by contrasting item with item as the preacher goes along: sin versus God as paymasters, wages versus gift, and death versus life. The second option would be to follow the outline as given, painting a dark picture of sin and its consequences, and ending with the bright hope of redemption and reward by choosing God and life.

7. The Chapter Outline Method.

An entire chapter may be chosen as a text, and it has many advantages. Generally, Bible chapters are divided logically, and most have a definable theme. Usually a short chapter serves our purpose better than a long one.

Example: a sermon outline from the first Psalm.
A specific sample of synthesized sermons from significant Psalms.

"The Two Ways"

A. The Blessed Man. Vs 1-3
    1. What he does not do.
        a. Walketh not.
        b. Standeth not.
        c. Sitteth not.
    2. What he does.
        a. His delight.
        b. His meditation.

3. His resulting life.
   a. Nature.
   b. Fruit.
   c. Work.

B. The ungodly Man (vs. 4-5)
   1. What he doesn't do.
      a. His walking --"not so".
      b. His standing -- "not so"
      c. His sitting -- "not so"
   2. What he does.
      a. His delight -- "Not so".
      b. His meditation -- "Not so".
   3. His resulting character.
      a. "Chaff".
      b. "Wind driveth away".

C. Their lifestyle and destination (vs. 6)
   1. The way of the righteous -- "The Lord knoweth".
   2. The way of the ungodly -- "Perish".

(Note: This is just one of the methods of presenting an expository sermon)

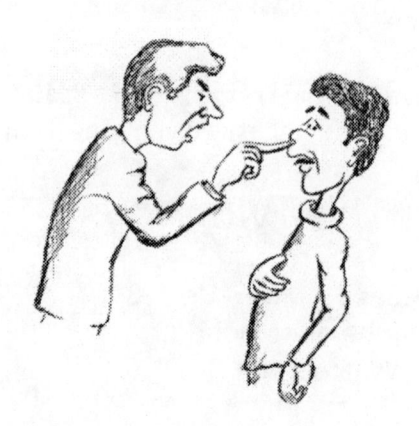

8. The Verse Outline Method

Two or more verses sometimes follow each other in such a manner as to suggest a natural sermon outline.
A text that works well as an outline is found in Romans 1:14-16.
The sermon outline is seen in a moment as one reads these verses.
The three "I am's" serve as corresponding clauses.

"I Am"
- I am debtor.
- I am ready.
- I am not ashamed.

Here is the sermon outline from Romans 1:14-16 further developed.

"Paul the Missionary"

A. I am debtor.
  1. To the Greeks.
  2. To the Barbarians.

B. I am ready.
  1. With resources.
  2. To seize the opportunity.

C. I am not ashamed.
  1. Because the Gospel is good news.
  2. Because the Gospel is powerful.

Another example comes from Philippians 4:11-13

"Through Christ"
- ☐ I have learned.
- ☐ I know how.
- ☐ I can do.

9. The Phrase Outline Method

Outlining a sermon by phrases applies the same principles as the word outline method. Usually short texts are used with "word" method but longer ones are necessary for phrase outline.

Example: I Thessalonians 1:9-10

Take the last part of verse 9 and first part of verse 10:

> *"Ye turned to God from idols, to serve the living and true God and to wait for His Son from heaven."*

This passage divides into three phrases as follows:

1. Ye turned to God from idols.
2. To serve the living and true God.
3. And wait for His Son from heaven.

After you have analyzed the text, the next step is to devise a method to correlate the three phrases about one common idea. Get the phrases and what they mean clearly in mind by setting them in writing. As you prayerfully wait on God, find connecting links that set the three phrases in logical order.

Sermon Outline

"The Tenses of the Christian Life".

    A. The past tense -- "ye turned".
        1. The positive turn -- "to God".
        2. The negative turn -- "from idols".

    B. The present tense -- "to serve".
        1. The social motive -- "living".
        2. The moral motive -- "true".

    C. The future tense -- "to wait"
        1. The one awaited -- "His Son"

2. The place whence awaited -- "heaven"

 D. Conclusion

Chapter 12

From the Apostle's Pen

**Exhortations from the Apostle Paul
to his spiritual son, Pastor Timothy**

From I Timothy 1

4. "(Do not) give heed to fables and endless genealogies, which minister questions, rather than godly edifying which is in faith, so do.
5. Now the end of the commandment is charity out of a pure heart, and of a good conscience, and of faith unfeigned,

> Paraphrased:
> The objective of preaching God's word is to teach and inspire the people to develop
> (1) love out of a pure heart,
> (2) a conscience that is sensitive to the Spirit, and
> (3) real faith, not just a show. [83]

6. From which some having turned aside unto vain jangling;
7. Desiring to be teacher of the law; understanding neither what they say, nor whereof they affirm.

---
[83] E. Weaver paraphrase

From I Timothy 4

6. If thou put the brethren in remembrance of these things, thou shalt be a good minister of Jesus Christ, nourished up in the words of faith and of good doctrine, whereunto thou hast attained.
7. But refuse profane and old wives' fables, and exercise thyself rather unto godliness.
12. Let no man despise thy youth; but be thou an example of the believers, in word, in conversation , in charity, in spirit, in faith, in purity.
13. Till I come, give attendance to reading, to exhortation, to doctrine.
14. Neglect not the gift that is in thee, which was given thee by prophecy, with the laying on of the hands of the presbytery.
15, Meditate upon these things; give thyself wholly to them; that thy profiting may appear to all.
16. Take heed unto thyself, and unto the doctrine; continue in them: for in doing this thou shalt both save thyself, and them that hear thee.

From I Timothy 6

17 Charge them that are rich in this world, that they be not high-minded, nor trust in uncertain riches, but in the living God, who giveth us richly all things to enjoy;
18 That they do good, that they be rich in good works, ready to distribute, willing to communicate;
19. Laying up in store for themselves a good foundation against the time to come, that they may lay hold on eternal life.
20. Oh, Timothy, keep that which is committed to thy trust, avoiding profane and vain babblings, and oppositions of science falsely so called;
21. Which some professing have erred concerning the faith.

From II Timothy 1

6. Wherefore I put thee in remembrance that thou stir up the gift of God, which is in thee by the putting on of my hands.
7. For God hath not given us the spirit of fear; but of power, and of love, and of a sound mind.
11. ...I am appointed a preacher, and an apostle, and a teacher of the Gentiles.
12. For the which cause I also suffer these things; nevertheless I am not ashamed: for I know whom I have believed, and am persuaded that he is able to keep that which I have committed unto him against that day.
13. Holding fast the form of sound words, which thou hast heard of me, in faith and love which is in Christ Jesus.

From II Timothy 2

1. Thou therefore, my son, be strong in the grace that is in Christ Jesus.
2. And the tings that thou hast heard of me among many witnesses, the same commit thou to faithful men, who shall be able to teach others also.
3. Thou therefore endure hardness, as a good soldier of Jesus Christ.
4. No man that warreth entangleth himself with the affairs of this life; that he may please him who hath called him to be a soldier.
14. Of these things put them in remembrance, charging them before the Lord that they strive not about words to no profit, but to the subverting of the hearers.
15. Study to shew thyself approved unto God, a workman that needeth not to be ashamed, rightly dividing the word of truth.
16. But shun profane and vain babblings: for they will increase unto more ungodliness.
24. And the servant of the Lord must not strive, but be gentle unto all men, apt to teach, patient,
25. In meekness instructing those that oppose themselves; if God peradventure will give them repentance to the acknowledging of the truth.

From II Timothy 3

14. But continue thou in the things which thou hast learned and hast been assured of, knowing of whom thou hast learned them;
15. And that from a child thou hast known the holy scriptures, which are able to make thee wise unto salvation through faith which is in Christ Jesus.
16. **All scripture is given by inspiration of God, and is profitable for doctrine, for reproof, for correction, for instruction in righteousness;**
17. **That the man of God may be perfect, throughly furnished unto all good works.**

From II Timothy 4

2. Preach the word; be instant in season, out of season; reprove, rebuke, exhort with all longsuffering and doctrine.
3. For the time will come that they will not endure sound doctrine; bu after their own lusts shall they heap to themselves teachers, having itching ears;
4. And they shall turn away their ears from the truth, and shall be turned unto fables.
5. But watch thou in all things, endure afflictions, do the work of an evangelist, make full proof of thy ministry.

Exhortations from Other Letters by Paul

From Romans I

11. For I long to see you, that I may impart unto you some spiritual gift, to the end ye may be established.
15. So as much as in me is, I am ready to preach the gospel to you that are at Rome also.
16. For I am not ashamed of the gospel of Christ: for it is the power of God unto salvation to every one that believeth; to the Jew first, and also to the Greek.
17. For therein is the righteousness of God revealed from faith to faith: as it is written, The just shall live by faith.

From Romans 10

17. So then faith cometh by hearing, and hearing by the word of God.

From I Corinthians 1

22. For the Jews require a sign, and the Greeks seek after wisdom:
23. But we preach Christ crucified, unto the Jews a stumblingblock, and unto the Greeks foolishness;
26. For ye see your calling, brethren, how that not many wise men after the flesh, not many mighty, not many noble, are called:
27. But God hath chosen the foolish things of the world to confound the wise; and God hath chosen the weak things of the world to confound the things which are mighty;
29. That no flesh should glory in his presence.

From I Corinthians 2

1. And I, brethren, when I came to you, came not with excellency of speech or of wisdom, declaring unto you the testimony of God.
2. For I determined not to know anything among you, save Jesus Christ, and Him crucified.
4. And my speech and my preaching was not with enticing words of man's wisdom, but in demonstration of the Spirit and of power:
5. That your faith should not stand in the wisdom of men, but in the power of God.
6. Howbeit we speak wisdom among them that are perfect: yet not the wisdom of this world...
7. But we speak the wisdom of God in a mystery...
12. Now we have received, not the spirit of the world, but the spirit which is of God; that we might know the things that are freely given to us of God.
13. Which things also we speak, not in the words which man's wisdom teacheth, but which the Holy Ghost teacheth; comparing spiritual things with spiritual.

From I Corinthians 4

18. Now some are puffed up, as though I would not come to you.
19. But I will come to you shortly, if the Lord will, and will know, not the speech of them which are puffed up, but the power.

From I Corinthians 9

16. For though I preach the gospel, I have nothing to glory of: for necessity is laid upon me; yea, woe is me if I preach not the gospel!

From II Corinthians 3

5. ...our sufficiency is of God;
6. Who also hath made us able ministers of the new testament; not of the letter, but of the spirit: for the letter killeth, but the spirit giveth life.

From II Corinthians 4

1. Therefore seeing we have this ministry, as we have received mercy, we faint not;
2. But have renounced the hidden things of dishonesty, not walking in craftiness, nor handling the word of God deceitfully; but by manifestation of the truth commending ourselves to every man's conscience in the sight of God.
5. For we preach not ourselves, but Christ Jesus the Lord; and ourselves your servants for Jesus' sake.
6. For God...hath shined in our hearts, to give the light of the knowledge of the glory of God in the face of Jesus Christ.
7. But we have this treasure in earthen vessels, that the excellency of the power may be of God, and not of us.

From II Corinthians 10

20. Now then we are ambassadors for Christ, as though God did beseech you by us: we pray you in Christ's stead, be ye reconciled to God.

HOMILETICS I

Annotated Bibliography

Compiled by:

Sylvia J. Imler, BS, MS, MTS

ANNOTATED BIBLIOGRAPHY

Barth, Karl. Homiletics. Louisville, KY: Westminster/John Knox Press, 1991.
    This revised edition gives the reader additional material not found in Barth's earlier work, "Homiletik." A more systematic order of presentation is provided. However, Barth strongly suggests that the introduction and conclusion be omitted from sermons as well as some other helps that today's minister may incorporate into his/her sermons. Within this text, the reader will observe how Barth attacks the îrelevanceî of preaching to societyís situations and needs. He believes the preacher should be Biblical -- let the Scriptures speak God's Word. Barth claims that preaching is nothing more than theology.

Blackwood, Andrew Watterson. Expository Preaching for Today: Case Studies of Bible Passages. New York: Abingdon-Cokesbury Press, 1953.

    This book, written for the pastor and the student, concerns itself with one type of Biblical preaching. Practically all of the cases in this writing deal with Bible passages. Each case is developed just enough to make the idea clear, but the author does suggest a path to follow if one desires to dig deeper. By using topics from the Bible, principles are brought out more or less inductively.

Broadus, John A. On the Preparation and Delivery of Sermons, 4th edition. New York: Harper San Francisco, 1979.
    This text is one of the most complete books for the study of homiletics with a wealth of basic material. This fourth edition has added material more contemporary, thus deleting some dated material. The contents were rearranged to conform to the usual sermon-building task. This book also directs the readerís attention to a diverse range of homiletical literature.

Brooks, Phillips. The Joy of Preaching. Grand Rapids: Kregel Publications, 1989.

Brooks focuses in on the essential principles of preaching. This book consists of a series of lectures which will enable the reader to understand and apply the basic principles and skills of homiletics. If the reader can experience what Phillips Brooks would desire for all ministers of the Gospel to experience, he/she will experience the joy of preaching.

Calkins, Raymond. The Eloquence of Christian Experience. New York: The Macmillan Co., 1927.

Calkins writes of the Christian experience in the quest for certainty, knowledge, and theology. He gives attention to the ipreacherî and the Christian experience as well as the Christian pastor and the Christian experience. The author then informs the reader how to cultivate the Christian experience. Calkins presents a series of thought-provoking questions to the reader and he provides possible solutions.

Davis, Ozora S. Principles of Preaching. Chicago: The University of Chicago Press, 1924.

This book is designed to be a textbook to present the principles of preaching which are abstracted from typical sermons. The sermons chosen were primarily to observe the homiletical method within them and also because there was a diversity of thought and temper prevalent. Types represented are the evangelistic, pastoral, dogmatic, and hortatory.

Demaray, Donald E. Introduction to Homiletics, 2nd edition. Grand Rapids: Baker Book House, 1990.

The author wrote this book as a textbook for men and women new in preaching. It can also be considered a textbook for the experienced preacher. This book is a recent publication for keeping the busy pastor informed and going deeper. This text draws from the classical tradition of homiletics from Augustine to the present.

Evans, Gillian R. The Art of Preaching. Kalamazoo, Michigan: Cistercian Pub., Inc., 1981.

This book is a translation of Alanus de Insulis, a scholar and religious man who died in 1202. This particular writing is one of Alanís works of practical theology. Motives for preaching, and the frame of mind of the preacher are addressed. The need for the preacher to modify the sermon to the audience is given attention as well. The Art of Preaching satisfies the scholastic desire for order, preciseness, and meticulousness. It is an explanation of the theory of composing sermons of the late twelfth century.

Evans, William. <u>How to Prepare Sermons</u>. Chicago: Moody Press, 1964.

This is a practical book which provides ministers, theological students, and laymen with helpful ideas of ministry. It does not attempt to give an exhaustive examination of homiletics, but rather a clearly outlined path for study, selection of texts for sermons and themes, and the construction of sermons.

Kinlaw, Dennis F. <u>Preaching in the Spirit</u>. Grand Rapids: Francis Asbury Press, 1985.

This book is full of energy and conviction. The preacherís life should be touched deeply through his/her communion with God. This book contains lectures prepared by Kinlaw. As the reader reads Preaching in the Spirit, he will be intrigued by the author's passion for ministering the Word of God.

Knott, H. E. <u>How to Prepare a Sermon</u>. Cincinnati: The Standard Press, 1927.

This manuscript was written for the express purpose of providing a brief, helpful approach to the science of sermon composition on correct homiletical principles. Questions are given at the conclusion of each chapter to promote discussion for study groups and training classes.

Knox, John. <u>The Integrity of Preaching</u>. New York: Abingdon Press, 1952.

John Knox defines and discusses Biblical preaching and its purpose. He describes preaching as a great art, the criteria for which cannot be concisely and exhaustively formulated. The relevance of preaching is discussed as well as other aspects of preaching: teaching, personal, worship, and sacrament.

Luccock, Halford E. Communicating the Gospel. New York: Harper & Brothers, Pub., 1954.

This manuscript consists of a series of the Lyman Beecher Lectures on Preaching at Yale University in April, 1953. Titles of lectures are: "A Babel of Tongues," "The faith Once Delivered -- Yesterday and Today," "To Serve the Present Age," "He Opened the Book," "The Preacher as Craftsman," and "Preaching During An Earthquake."

Macartney, Clarence Edward. Preaching Without Notes. New York: Abingdon-Cokesbury Press, 1956.

The author has drawn from his forty-one years of experience in the pulpit to prepare this text. He speaks to theological students, ministerial gatherings, and conferences through the themes of the chapters. Four of the chapters were delivered at the Princeton Institute of Theology. This book was not designed to be a textbook on homiletics, but an account of the author's personal experience in study and preparation in preaching.

Macpherson, Ian. The Art of Illustrating Sermons. New York: Abingdon Press, 1964.

The Art of Illustrating Sermons is a book designed to show the reader how to observe, sort, research, store, and use illustrations in sermons. Many examples are used to demonstrate the practical use of illustrations within the sermon in order for the message to be more effective.

Montgomery, R. Ames. Expository Preaching. New York: Fleming H. Revell Co., 1939.

The purpose of this book is to encourage the preacherís interest in the study of the Bible so that the people's understanding of the Scriptures may improve and the preacher's message may become more effective and pertinent to present needs. Lectures are presented to better illustrate expository preaching.

Pattison, T. Harwood. <u>The Making of the Sermon</u>. Philadelphia: The American Baptist Publication Society, 1941.

    This book was primarily written for the use of the student in the classroom. This book will also be instrumental in informing ministers who have not taken any seminary courses. The definition of preaching is discussed along with guidelines to sermon preparation. Also included are rhetorical elements in the sermon.

Perry, Lloyd M. <u>Biblical Preaching for Todayís World</u>. Revised. Chicago: Moody Press, 1990.

    This book is designed to provide concepts, structures, and resources essential for effective preaching of the Bible. This text identifies the foundations and Biblical bases for preaching, logical organizational approaches to preaching, and techniques that will allow variety to preaching with the purpose of enhancing the listener's interest level. This book is practical in helping preachers become effective Biblical communicators.

Reid, Clyde. <u>The Empty Pulpit</u>: A Study in Preaching As Communication. New York: Harper & Row Pub., 1967.

    Reid refers to the empty pulpit as lacking in meaning and relevance and a failure to communicate. This book has attempted to break through some of the theological jargon. The purpose of this manuscript is to encourage dialogue on this subject and to observe it more realistically. A contrast between preaching and communication is given.

Robinson, Haddon W. <u>Biblical Preaching: The Development and Delivery of Expository Messages</u>. Grand Rapids: Baker Book House, 1980.

    This is a basic text for the student or pastor who desires the fundamentals of Biblical preaching. The author's style is informal but practical in its purpose. Exercises are included to reinforce homiletical principles. Robinson gives precise definitions. This book was designed for the student, minister, and layman.

Rust, Eric C. <u>The Word and Words: Towards a Theology of Preaching</u>. Macon, Georgia: Mercer University Press, 1982.

This book was birthed out of a series of lectures given by the author. The purpose of this text was to help make the speaker's words more effective and relevant when preaching the Gospel. It is extremely important that thoughts are communicated with clarity.

Tizard, Leslie J. Preaching: <u>The Art of Communication</u>. New York: Oxford University Press, 1959.

This book is based on a series of lectures given by Leslie Tizard. When writing this book Tizard had theological students and beginning preachers in mind. The author's personal experiences and conception of the preacherís calling are included in this text: "What Preaching Is"; "The Personality of the Preacher"; "The Art of Communication"; and "Pastoral Preaching" are the chapter topics.

Bibliography

Bible Study Methods

Eberhardt, Charles. The Bible in the Making of Ministers.
    New York: Association Press, 1949.

Gettys, Joseph M. Teaching Pupils How to Study the Bible.
    Richmond: John Knox Press, 1950.

Jensen, Irving L. Independent Bible Study. Chicago: Moody Press, 1963.

Tenny, Merrill C. The Genius of the Gospels. Grand Rapids:

    William B. Eerdmans Publishing Co., 1951. (See also his book of Galations).

Traina, Robert. Methodical Bible Study. Privately published, 1952.

Vos, Howard. Effective Bible Study, 2nd edition.
    Grand Rapids: Zondervan Publishing House, 1956.

Biblical Hermeneutics

Mickelson, A. Berkeley. Interpreting the Bible. Grand Rapids:
    William B. Eerdmans Publishing Company, 1963.

Terry, Milton. Biblical Hermeneutics. Grand Rapids:
    Zondervan Publishing House, n.d.

Homiletics

Knott, Harold E. How to Prepare Expository Sermons. Cincinnati:
    The Standard Publishing Company, 1930.

Ray, Jeff D. Expository Preaching.

Reu, M. Homiletics: A Manual of the Theory and Practice of Preaching.
    Pages 319-320 ff., 323 f., 428. Baker Book House, 1967.

Unger, Merrill F. Principles of Expository Preaching.
    Grand Rapids: Zondervan Publishing House, 1955.

Humor

Weaver, Ernest Church People Funny Side Up   Weaver Publishing 1991
    Weaver Publishing, 1127 Brittany Place, Fort Wayne, IN 46825